Breathe
A Memoir

DARRELL FOSTER

Omega Press
PO Box 91659
Pasadena, CA 91109

Ordering Information:

Quantity sales. Special discounts are available on quantity purchases by corporations, associations, and others. For details, contact the publisher at the address above.

Orders by U.S. trade bookstores and wholesalers. Please contact the publisher at the address above, or call 661.775.9025

Printed in the United States of America

Publisher's Cataloging-in-Publication data Foster, Darrell
Breathe : a memoir / Darrell Foster

ISBN: 9781549935138

First Edition

CONTENTS

Dedicated to my beautiful children -

Darrell Foster, Jr., Keeana Foster, Giovanni Foster, and Bella Foster.

FOREWORD

According to the old saying, "Everybody is running from something."

Let's make a little tweak to that: "Everybody is running *for* something." And that something is specific to each and every one of us; it's what pushes us through those middle miles, and fills us with pride when the treadmill blinks, "Great job" at the end of a workout. Running with Darrell Foster wasn't the first time I ran—but it was the first time I realized I was running for something more than a bottle of water and a hot shower. But before I get into all that, there's something you should know about me: I can't take full credit for having Ali's punches down pat. I didn't get those vampire-killing abs for *I Am Legend* all by myself. I had someone pushing me every single step of the way, a man I'm proud to call my coach, in life and in the gym: Darrell Foster. I call him "D"—and I'm honored to be able to call him one of my closest friends.

You might've picked up this book thinking it holds the secrets to Your Best Body Ever or has recipes for a healthy, low-carb diet. But that's not what this is. *Breathe* is Darrell's heart and soul printed on paper. It's a crushingly honest memoir that illuminates one man's struggle against life's unrelenting obstacles, and how he outran, outsmarted, and outclassed his circumstances, detractors, and demons. Simply put, Breathe is a recipe for success. The same way that Joseph Campbell's "Hero's journey" guides writers on the steps their Hero must take to bring the elixir back to the Ailing Kingdom, Darrell's narration of his tests, trials, enemies, and allies is a roadmap for those journeying to become the greatest version of themselves. Anybody who has trained with D knows how lofty his expectations are, how demanding a session can be. Funny thing is, life is the same way. Life won't give us a few seconds to catch our breath or to find an easier way; life comes at us whenever it feels like it, and we better be prepared. Like D says: "Don't get ready—*stay* ready."

Darrell's anecdotes of personal tragedy and triumph illuminate a fundamental concept of our reality: that the tiniest sliver of light will shine through even the deepest darkness. For D, that light was Reading and Running. Darrell increased his stamina so he could fortify his body against attacks from without. He ingested centuries of knowledge to fortify his mind against doubt and self-hatred, the viruses festering within. When given the choice between success and surrender, Darrell rose to the challenge and went through the fire, in order to become the person the universe needed him to be. To see Darrell where he is today—a businessman, an author, a wonderful father—is a testament to the truth of his principles and the enduring strength of his vision. But D can't take full credit for his success, either. Every Hero has a Mentor. When Darrell needed it most, he saw the light, heard the voice, and knew what he had to do: breathe. Fill himself with a positive attitude and a passion for all the things that life had to offer—not all that life had taken from him. And look at the man he has become, the story he's decided to share with us all.

What do I run for? My family. My films. My fitness. And I run for my friend, my mentor, Darrell Foster.

I've known D for a long time, but I didn't truly know him until I read Breathe. Now, I love him even more.

- *Will Smith*

PROLOGUE: TREAD LIGHTLY

If you're training to become a Warrior, you should feel a barely- describable intensity in everything you do: the running, the eating, the stretching, the punching—everything.

What people don't realize is that it's even more intense for the coach, the one responsible for the training. Not only does the coach have to endure everything the future Warrior must, but he has to be a cheerleader, a teacher, a psychiatrist, an internist, a sounding board, a taskmaster, and a friend.

I'm the Coach. And in 2000, my coaching was about to be put to its toughest test: I'd been commissioned to transform Will Smith, arguably Hollywood's biggest movie star, into Muhammad Ali. There would be no pretending Ali. Will Smith had to *become* him.

When I'm training somebody to become a Warrior, I always lead by example, and this job was no different. I worked—and I mean worked—alongside Will in preparation for his role, maintaining the level of fitness required of a professional fighter. I made it clear that this was a fighter's training camp, not an actor's training camp.

Our typical day started at 6:00 A.M. with a three-to-five mile run, then at 11:30, it was two-and-a-half-hours of boxing training. At 3:00 p.m., we watched old fight films, and not just footage of Ali, but Sugar Ray Leonard, Joe Louis, Willie Pep, and Sugar Ray Robinson. All this diversity of style and era helped Will live and breathe boxing; he needed to see the old arenas and understand what it was like to be the main event. At 5:00 PM, we did weight training, which was key, because I only had one year to put thirty pounds of muscle on Will's slender frame.

I set up our training camp in the snow-capped Rocky Mountains of Aspen, 8,000 feet above sea level. Why? Because the higher you get in the atmosphere, the less oxygen is present, which places extreme pressure on the mind and body of the athlete in training. I needed Will to be in exceptionally adverse conditions, because I had to do everything in my power to transform him into a world class fighter. The adverse conditions were designed to simulate what the mind and body goes through during a fifteen round bout. Will had to learn what it felt like to be getting his ass beat. You can't breathe. Your lungs are on fire. You are being attacked from every angle. It's like you are in a cage with a ferocious lion who wants nothing more than to rip your body to shreds.

We were far from all the glamour, the "lights-camera-action" of Hollywood. Out there, it was primal. It was about survival, about becoming a real boxer. To be a professional fighter, Will was going to have to dig deep and give it his all, because real fighters fight to get out of the ghetto, or to provide food for their family each night, and he was an internationally revered film star. It was going to take everything inside of him and more to accomplish this monumental task.

The early morning in question was the kind of morning where you wake up feeling like you have only slept for half an hour, but regardless of the way we felt, we had to lace up the combat boots and get to work. After we stepped out of our warm hotel rooms and met one another on the hotel's porch, the blistering Colorado wind ripped through our clothes, penetrating to the marrow in our bones. It felt as if every hair on the back of my neck was reaching out, grabbing hold of the frigid air and blowing it down the spine of my back. The snow covered the ground around us, creating blankets of billowy mush. As the wind swirled about, we could barely see each other. When I took the first step off of the porch, my foot plunged knee deep into the pure white downy snow. "Shit," I mumbled to myself, "this is going to be hard." But before my mind went too far in that negative direction, I remembered my responsibility to the legacy of Ali, and that it's hard even for the best of them.

To be the best in the world, you must sacrifice and suffer. One can only know and appreciate good if there is some conceptual understanding of evil. To fully appreciate peace, you have to know turmoil. You have to be above reproach and set the example for everyone else. Life provides the circumstantial elements, but it's up to you to decide what you will do with what you have been given. There are no excuses.

As Will and I ran our daily miles in the high, rigid mountains of Aspen, I again considered my job: to represent all that Ali stood for and fought to defend. We were taking on a seemingly insurmountable task, but we were ready to pay the price because too much was on the line. It was up to us, and us alone. I knew that when the time came for Will to play Ali, it wouldn't matter that the training was hard or that we were tired or that we had to travel and train for days, weeks, and months away from home. Critics, filmgoers, friends, acquaintances, and even family wouldn't allow for there to be any gaps between who Ali was and who Will was. He had to make a real transformation not only for the legacy he represented, but for the sake of his professional career as well.

We ground through the difficult terrain, putting one foot in front of the other, destroying any mental barricades. Our breathing was labored, our intestinal fortitude was tested. I took the lead, sprinting a few paces in front of Will, leading by example, challenging him to keep stride with me, knowing this is what makes a Warrior in the ring. After a few minutes, I stopped feeling his presence behind me. I turned, and there, about ten yards back, Will was resting on one knee in the snow.

I flashed back to 1970: Muhammad Ali vs. Oscar Bonavena, and thought, That's the punch! That's when Bonavena stunned Ali with a left hook to the jaw in the ninth round. That's what Will has got to learn. The pain he feels now, like he is about to die—this is exactly where he needs to be. Because of the dense fog that surrounded us, I couldn't see Will's face. All that was visible was the air we were exhaling, in which I saw ghosts of fighters past, faces of old fighters manifesting themselves through the thick fog. It was like Will had been hit with a body shot from Joe Louis, whose ghost was engulfing his body. The fact that he had reached this point excited me.

I yelled, "GET UP MOTHAFUCKA! GET UP! THIS IS WHAT IT TOOK FOR ALI TO BE CHAMP." Before Will could respond, I yelled, "AND WHILE YOU'RE DOWN THERE, WRITE HIS NAME! WRITE ALI IN THE SNOW!"

The laws of nature were working against Will's body and mind. Gravity wanted to keep him down. The limited amount of oxygen made breathing almost impossible. Tears came to my eyes, freezing before they could fall off my face, because of this great responsibility. It wasn't really about me and boxing: it was about great men who will stand up to challenges; it was about discovering I was somebody.

At that moment, I felt close to God. When you are on the right path, you know it. You become the person you were created to be. You start to acknowledge the God within you. The weight of my duty rested heavily on my shoulders.

Because I, and I alone, had to turn this man into a Warrior.

1

AM I WORTHY OF MY SUFFERING

The year was 1963. I was five years old.

There I was again, lying awake in my bed, my heart pounding like deafening drums, filling the silent void in my ears. Beads of sweat dripped down the sides of my head and I felt the moisture of anxiety soak into my faded baby blue t-shirt, the same shirt I had had on for the past three days. My chest screamed in pain, and I could barely breathe. My tongue was stuck to the top of my mouth and I swallowed hard as my throat welled in terror. I squeezed my eyes shut as tight as I possibly could and shivered, not because it was cold, but because I was terrified.

I heard it coming down the hallway, stomping towards me. The force of each step shook the house and rattled the thin walls that separated me from this horrific noise. Through hushed whispers, I prayed, "Please God, no. Not tonight." And then, suddenly, the sound stopped. The rattling dishes in the kitchen balanced to a quiet silence, and I, too, froze as I held my breath and listened carefully for a few seconds. Just as quickly as the stomping stopped, it started again, and I let out a soft whimper, tensed my shoulders, and suppressed the knot that wound tightly in my gut. With each passing second, the longer I waited, the more terrified I became.

In this pitch-black room, my eyes clamped shut, my other senses screamed in fear of what was looming outside my door. I smelled the scent of whiskey and cigarettes. I heard the rumbling, drunk voices from the other side of the house. As the sound moved closer, my ears registered what I'd been praying to God I wouldn't hear: the doorknob. I cringed as the squeaking filled my room.

The room was void of all light and I couldn't see a thing. What time is it? I wondered. I had been asleep for what felt like only five minutes, but surely it had been longer than that. I grimaced, rolled into a fetal position, and pretended to be asleep.

Suddenly, like a flash of lightning raging across the dark sky, all I could see were colorless dots flashing like a strobe light, screaming for attention. As the sensation of pain wrapped around my senses, I gasped for air as all of the colors of God's rainbow vanished from my reality. With my eyes now wide open, I could only decipher darkness, pitch black dotted with white sparks of pain.

I wailed at the top of my lungs, "Stop—*please*—*no*—stop!" Unrelenting, it went on for what seemed like an eternity in my five-year-old mind.

The lash of the orange extension cord ripped through my skin as if I were made of paper mache. My skin crackled as the whip exploded my flesh, revealing the vulnerable, raw tissue of my body. I prayed to God to make it stop, screaming as the whip shredded my skin. Showing no mercy, showing nothing but complete and utter hatred for my existence, the beating continued.

Whip after whip, the sound of the extension cord whistling through the air faded into a quiet hum as I slipped into dark unconsciousness. My mind was protecting my body; I was supposed to survive this. At five, I felt like I'd lived and suffered thousands of deaths, one hundred of them on this very night. Although there were other people around, there was no one there who would hear my cries, who would rescue me or save me from it, from this Monster, for the one whose role as rescuer this should be was the one holding the whip to kill my soul.

This Monster was my mother.

My childhood was a living hell, and the absurdity of what I had to deal with, what I had to overcome is almost incomprehensible. On a regular basis, I would get beaten out of my sleep, verbally abused, pushed to the limits of human endurance, and from my mother, all I heard was a litany of, "You ain't shit and ain't never gonna be shit."

To be alive simply meant I had to survive.

I had nobody to protect me. My father left when I was a baby, disappearing from any responsibility, leaving me without the protection that most fathers offer to their children. (In my neighborhood, it wasn't uncommon to have single parent homes with the mothers having sole responsibility for raising their children.) I knew very little about the man who people called my father, but I do know that he was one of the best first baseman the game of baseball has ever known. I'd be out and about in town and people on the streets would call out to me, "Hey! You're Foster's boy, huh? He was the best baseball player I'd ever seen." Although I didn't know him, I still welled up with intense pride at my father's legacy, even if the legacy was only on the streets of my hometown. But his baseball greatness did nothing to protect me from the whims of my abusive mother. She was not only my torturer, but she held the double life of a God-fearing, religious, good hearted, police officer! She was the law! Who could I call? Who was I going to tell? Who could I call to save me?

Even if I could muster the courage to mention the abuse to someone outside of my home, it would never be accepted or believed. My mother was involved in the community. Aside from her seemingly good deeds as a police officer, she and I went to church twice a week, every Sunday and every Wednesday, to the United House of Prayer. I didn't understand too much of what was going on at church, with people shouting, screaming, and babbling under the guise of "speaking in tongues." However, in Sunday school, I did learn about God and the love that He shows to his children— but I just couldn't understand how that was possible in a situation like mine. I figured that God stuff just wasn't meant for me. My mom was such a believer that she blared religious songs like Shirley Caesar's "No Charge" throughout our roach-infested, abuse-filled, sexually-promiscuous life-hole that I was forced to call home. I grew to hate those songs. In fact, I grew to hate everything else that reminded me of her.

Where is this God that I hear so much about? I'd wonder. Lord this, Lord that. It just doesn't make sense.

My mother was from a coal miner's family and I'm sure she had had her deal of pain and suffering too. I know her past and her childhood had a major part in contributing to her torturing me. Looking back, I can see the how the cycle of ignorance played out over and over, and would continue to do so until someone made a conscious choice to live life differently.

However, that was no excuse and I regarded her actions against me as most evil.

The year was 1965. I was seven years old.

It was a Wednesday night. The damp summer air slithered into the house under the cracks of the floor and through the broken windows that lined the walls. The rolling thunder and fierce lightning that struck the sky provided a sense of wonder and peace as I sat staring out of the window in my bedroom. Sitting cross-legged on my bed, a slightly tattered twin mattress on the wooden floor of the room, I could see my reflection in the broken windowpane as the light of the bright moon descended from the sky. Suddenly, I heard loud noises coming from my mother's bedroom. It sounded like talking, chuckling, screaming, and yelling. I wondered, *Why are there so many men in the house? What are they doing?* My mother was simultaneously screaming and laughing; it sounded as if someone was hurting her. I burst into her bedroom, and there was a man on top her. He wasn't a huge man, but he had my mother pinned face down on her bed, which was a slightly larger mattress than the one in my room. The sheets were strewn about and the pillows were bunched up at the foot of the mattress. I couldn't see the man's face because his back was turned toward the door, but I could see his knuckles turning white from the force he was using to hold down my mother's arms, which were outstretched above her head. She screamed again. Her voice was muffled, absorbed by the fabric of the mattress.

In a state of panic, I yelled, "Get off my mommy! Leave her alone!"

Snapping his head around to see me standing in the doorway, the man quickly rolled off of my mother, grabbed his shirt to cover his nakedness, and snatched the sheets from the floor. He yelled at my mother, "You left the damn door open?"

My mother jumped up, adjusted her house gown to cover herself, walked to me, and slapped me across my face as hard as she possibly could, sending my world into a spinning frenzy. I shook my head to collect myself, unsure of what had just happened. Out of the corner of my eye, I saw the ceiling fan whipping around and around, almost as if it were going to fly off of its hinges. The faint floral pattern on my mother's house gown looked like a psychedelic wave of colors. I stumbled to my right, trying to secure my footing, then looked up to the sight of her murderous brown eyes glaring down at me. Through gritted teeth, she said, "You'd better leave this bedroom, *now!*"

Confused and scared, I staggered into the kitchen and looked around for something that could help me save her. After a second, I caught a glimmer of chrome on the countertop. I took a couple steps backward and noticed two shiny gun belts perched just beyond my grasp. One belonged to a cop, the other to a mailman who I'd seen delivering the mail. At the tender age of six, I knew a lot about guns. Sometimes, when my mother was asleep, I'd hold her gun in my hand—its power always crawled up my arm, swelling my chest with confidence—and pretended to shoot the people who walked by the front door of our house. As the innocent people strolled along the sidewalk, I practiced my technique for the streets. The thugs in my neighborhood made gun slinging seem easy, and I looked up to those guys in the streets with guns. I wanted to be like them, not like the gun-wielding police officer my mother was to the world. I didn't realize that mailmen carried guns too, but I was sure that was indeed the mailman in my mother's bedroom.

I wondered, *What's he doing inside my house?*

I jumped and stretched my arm to grab the gun belts from the counter, but I couldn't get to it. I just couldn't reach it. I was getting more desperate by the second, but the thought of saving my mommy, and being her hero were driving me. I must save her! I must save my mommy!

And then, from behind me, a noise. Panicked, I turned around, and there she was. Just as I tried to explain what I was doing, her hand came down on the left side of my head, knocking me onto my back. My ears rang and my eyes crossed as my head bounced off of the linoleum. Standing over me, she screamed "Don't you get it? Leave me alone! Don't ever come into my room again," then turned around and hurried back into the bedroom, slamming the door behind her.

As I struggled to my feet, I blocked out the pain and wondered, *What are they doing?* She hated me, but I still wanted to save her from the man jumping up and down on her. I'm not sure what compelled me to burst into her room and make such a demand. After all, she never wanted to protect me. As quickly as I could gather myself, I ran from the kitchen through the front door and into the streets of my neighborhood. I wanted to leave, to get far away from everything.

The 7-Eleven wasn't too far from my house, so I figured I'd go hang out by the door until someone offered me a soda or a candy bar, which usually lifted my spirits. My friend Cozy sometimes came along and, every now and then, the manager would spot us from behind the counter and holler, "Get out of here boys!" Other times he would pretend he didn't see us at all.

As I ran toward the store, I noticed a shiny new bicycle sitting at the front door of Cozy's apartment. Nobody leaves his bike on the porch—or at least not if he intends for it to be there when he comes back outside—so I knew it hadn't been out there for long. I rushed up to the bicycle, swung my right leg over the seat, and moved the kickstand back with my left foot. I carefully rolled the bike past the open screen door and hollered, "Cozy! 7-Eleven, come on man!"

I saw Cozy sitting on the sofa, eating from a bag of potato chips. When he realized I was perched on top of his new bicycle, he bounded up from the sofa and exclaimed, "Darrell! That's my bike!" And the chase was on.

Speeding away, a devilish grin spread across my face. Looking back over my shoulder, I saw Cozy take off running after me. Laughing out loud, I said, "Catch me and you can have it back!"

Running full speed after the bike, Cozy said, "Hey man! Give me that bike back!" He chased me all the way to the store. My stomach hurt from laughing at him. I'd never seen Cozy get so worked up before.

Once he reached the store, he found the bike perched on its side, leaning against the wall. He yanked the bike up and stared at me with raw anger. I looked him in the eyes, trying to hold back the smirk that was creeping up on to the corners of my mouth. He said, "Man, why did you do that? Why you stole my bike?"

I said, "Man, it was a joke. You know that was funny."

Cozy's shoulders softened, and he let out a laugh, then admitted, "I just took that bike from Derrick's porch." He had stolen the bike himself, so it was hilarious that karma would come back around so quickly. We laughed together as we inspected the bike, looking at the shiny spokes, the fresh blue paint, the perfect wheels, and the amazing shocks. We looked up at each other and, at the same exact time, said, "I wonder who Derrick stole it from?" Busting our gut laughing, we decided we would share the newly acquired bike. That is, until someone stole it from us.

The year was 1966. I was eight years old.

It was a bright Sunday afternoon, a beautiful springtime day in D.C., and we were returning home from church. I was in the backseat of my mother's beige 1952 Cadillac Deville. The smoke from her Kool menthol cigarette filled my lungs, but I wasn't allowed to crack the window because the wind would upset her new, expensive hairdo.

As I stared out the window, I noticed the cherry blossom trees that lined the road back to our house. It was the first time I'd really noticed them, and they were everywhere, and I wondered where they came from, why they appeared all of a sudden. The white was almost blinding me. Pulling into the driveway, the sense of wonder evaporated and all the life and light diminished as I saw the front door of our house. I suddenly felt nauseated.

When we walked into the house, my mother slapped the back of my head and barked, "Hurry up and change those clothes, because a nasty animal like you doesn't belong in nice clothes like that. You ain't shit, boy!"

I hated those words. I hated her voice. I hated the way she spoke to me. Her voice felt like a million tiny needles stabbing my skin. I decided that if she didn't love me, I would love myself. I had to care about me, even if nobody else did.

I walked into my room, carefully removed my church clothes and folded them just so, tucking each corner with precision, because I knew that if I failed to meet her ungodly, impossible standards, I'd get hit, and I really didn't want to get beat again. I thought, *Maybe if I just do everything right, I won't get punished.* Carefully, I stacked my garments and changed into my favorite outdoor ensemble: a Washington Redskins t-shirt littered with holes, the logo faded beyond recognition. When I put it on, I felt like I could be myself. I loved the game of football and learned all I knew about the sport from my time playing two-hand touch with the dudes from the neighborhood.

Directly across the street from my apartment complex stood Kenny's shoe store, which boasted a huge parking lot lined with street lamps that lit up the lot at night. The lights were put in to keep thieves from breaking into the store at night, but to us, they meant football. It was like playing under the lights at Jack Kent Cooke Stadium, home of the Redskins: all you had to do was imagine the cheers from the thousands of fans roaring in the stadium around you.

There was one particular night of parking light football I'll never forget. A whole group of guys from the neighborhood were on the concrete slab that became our field of dreams, including Cozy, and Clifton and David Moore. Cozy was the quarterback and had an arm like a rocket. Me: I was the smallest kid on the team.

"Ready, hut!" called Clifton and the ball was snapped to Cozy. I took one look at my QB and knew his pass was coming straight at me. Taking off in a sprint toward our end zone, I turned my head to see the ball flying straight at me. I reached up, grabbed the spiraling ball, and tucked it under my right arm as I sped into the end zone. The team erupted in cheers, fist pumps, and exhilaration at what turned out to be the game-winning touchdown. I felt like a hero on the football field of Kenny's shoe store parking lot, and smiled as Cozy said, "Darrell is MVP for the night."

After we'd finish our games, we'd usually head to the 7-Eleven to get chips and soda. The MVP was always treated to free snacks. But that night was different. I had been planning this hero moment for some time and when my mother would send me to the store to buy groceries, I would keep some leftover food stamps, saving them for such a time as this. We walked into the store and before any of the guys could clamor to the chips and soda, I said "Free slurpies for everyone. On me, the MVP!" They all laughed and gladly filled their slurpy cups to the top.

That day after church, wearing that ragged Redskins t-shirt, nylon shorts, and tennis shoes, I snuck out of my bedroom window, a sense of freedom engulfing me. Shoulders tense, I took two cautious steps away from my house, in hopes that the Monster didn't see me leaving. With the coast clear, I exploded into a sprint, my small, four-foot frame moving like a king cheetah racing through the African desert at seventy miles per hour. My shoes didn't fit properly, but I ran. I ran as fast as I could move my legs.

The wind pressed against my face and my heart pounded as if my survival were dependent upon getting as far away from that house as was humanly possible. One foot hit the pavement, then the next—faster, harder, closer to my destination. Finally the Grand Tree—with its huge, wide arms and safe branches, branches that I knew would protect me from the Monster—was in my horizon.

I had a lot of secrets, and the Grand Tree was one of them. This was the place I could run to when I wanted to escape the realities of my world. I had plenty of good times, but the bad times were horrid, deafening, suffocating, and overwhelming. Feeling trapped by the dark secrets of my life, I felt that this tree provided a sense of security that nothing or nobody else could give me.

Whenever I was up in the branches of the Grand Tree, the view of the Earth below usually made me feel only a little stronger—but today was different. Today, I felt like I could have kept running for days. A part of me wishes that I'd never stopped to climb the tree that day. Perhaps I would have had to the courage to run away and never return. There was a sense of peace that overcame me when I ran, but the peace was fleeting because I knew that I had to go back home and attempt to avoid the Monster for the rest of the day. I was a prisoner of my own existence.

Having been reprimanded in the past for returning home past dusk, my instincts forced me home before the sun started to set—but why did I care so much? I would get beaten for no reason at all, so it wasn't like my obedience or disobedience ever affected the outcome of her wrath. Nonetheless, I returned home before dark.

I walked up the steps of my apartment. From outside, I heard the blasting record player. The sound was at maximum volume and, even though the singer's voice was cracking through the speakers, I was able to make out the words:

For the nine months I carried you, holding you inside me—
NO CHARGE.
For the night I sat up and doctored you and prayed for you—
NO CHARGE.
For the time and tears and the costs through the years there is
NO CHARGE.
When you add it all up the full cost of my love is
NO CHARGE.

The song consumed every square inch of our house. Hesitantly, I opened the front door and took two small steps inside. Before I had the chance to run for my life, I saw her out of the corner of my eye. I shook my head no, my bottom lip quivering in fear, as it dawned on me that she'd waited all day for me to return, probably thinking about what a nuisance I'd been, and what a curse to her life is my existence. She likely told herself stories about how she could have been beautiful and successful if it weren't for me in her life. If only she had chosen to have an abortion, her life would have been so different. She slowly rocked back and forth in the wooden chair, the floor creaking with every move.

When she saw me, she screamed "Come here" so loudly that her voice momentarily drowned out Shirley Caesar's. My eyes stared at her blankly and I felt the thick air of tension as the room closed in, suffocating me yet again. Reluctantly, slowly, and with a silent wish that it was all a horrible nightmare, my body stiffened as I walked towards her in anticipation of the inevitable blow to the head. I stopped about two feet in front of her, eyes to the ground and clamped shut, arms stiff at my side, fists clinched tight. She stood up from the chair and yanked my right arm towards her, pulling me within inches of her body. She shoved my face to the ground, then forcefully yanked my head between her legs and squeezed her thick powerful thighs around my neck. Circulation cut off, my eyes watered as I gasped for air. In an act of cruelty, she released just enough pressure for my mind to stay conscious.

And then, she unleashed the wrath.

She grabbed a black leather bull strap—a strap that she'd shortened in order to inflict maximum pain—pulled her arm back, and boom, the strap lashed through my skin. From between her legs, I screamed and thrashed, relentlessly trying to escape her grip. Using every ounce of force and might she could muster, she beat and whipped and slashed my back until my body went limp, and only then did she release her legs from my throat. My weak, bloodied, broken frame fell to the ground, completely numb.

My life was strangled and beaten out of me, and I couldn't react or retaliate. In that moment, I just wanted ultimate peace, to go to a place where I could be free from the pain and tortures of my life, a place without tears and heartache, a place where I would finally find love. I knew whatever was on the other side had to be better than this. All that I learned about Heaven and the afterlife flashed through my mind as my doubts of its truth melted into belief, forming wishful thoughts of dying and retreating to a peaceful place in the sky.

Waking up with bloodstained clothes, a swollen back of stripes, and pain almost too excruciating to define, I wondered, *What did I do to deserve this? I am so tired. I don't have to take this anymore.* When I came to, I vowed to myself that I would never cry again, because if I didn't, I wouldn't feel. No crying, no smiling, no laughing—absolutely no feeling. Where did laughs and smiles come from anyway? I really didn't even know.

In an effort of sheer will, I once again survived this experience. I knew it was up to me to save myself. I didn't give into the lies that tried to crawl into my ears, or the sound of hatred that flew from my mother's lips. I made a choice to think differently, to keep moving forward.

I later learned that the hatred my mother showed for me was meant for someone else. Turns out, I looked like the man who abused her. There were times that she would mutter his name under her breath before calling out mine. Every time she saw my face, she saw his face, and because of that similarity, she'd beat me out of my sleep, lash or strike me with whatever weapon she could find, without provocation. She hated me, and took out her pain and revenge and anger toward the universe on her child. It was worse than killing me, and I guess that gave her more satisfaction. I never found out who this mystery man was, but I have doubts that I'm really Robert Foster's son. It's more likely that I'm the child of the unknown man who raped and abused my mother.

This continued on for years, until I was big enough to defend myself. With each beating, with each instance of abuse, my skin thickened, my heart hardened, and walls of impenetrable steel erected themselves in my mind and soul. Little by little, the bigger I got, the stronger I got, both mentally and physically. I was determined not to be a product of her actions against me.

However strong I had become, I never really learned what "mommy" meant. I didn't know what it meant to have the woman who bore you to love you unconditionally, to have that person who will always protect and support you. I simply didn't share that reality with most of the world's population. Later in life, I would see war movies, and when people who were near death cried out for their mommas, I didn't understand why, in that moment of need, they wanted nothing more than the presence of their mother. This was the reality of my life, yet I had to put on an outward face of contentment because I could not run the risk of outing my mother. Anything I said would be constructed as a lie from a crazy kid.

Throughout my childhood, this had to be our secret, her secret. I went to church and went to school. I had to be a functioning part of her external world. She dressed me very well and made sure I was always immaculately groomed. She went to great lengths to hide any perception of dysfunction. However, underneath my classy clothes, behind my well-groomed body, there were bruises, and scars, and open wounds that were caused by her anger. My teachers thought I was autistic, or socially unstable because of the way I acted in class and in recreation time. I avoided most social interactions and stood by my vow to eradicate feelings from my life so nothing or nobody really would matter to me. Underneath the hard façade, I was dying from the excruciating pain. All I heard in my head were the threatening words of my mother: "You better not tell. You better not let anyone see you." So, I hid behind my pain and found solace in my running.

However, I knew I had a bigger purpose in this life. It was up to me to find out what.

2

BE THE LIGHT

The year was 1967. I was nine years old.

I may not have been big enough or strong enough to stop the abuse, but I was resilient, determined to keep moving forward.

During this time, I discovered a world that I didn't know existed: the world of running.

There was a space on this earth where I could escape the reality of my crazy world. I was a battered, beaten, abused nine-year-old boy running through the wind. When I ran, I was free. All the pressures and weight of the world were lifted from my shoulders, and it was during these moments of freedom that I could breathe.

I now had a secret that the Monster didn't know about. Running wasn't simply about the freedom of being uncatchable; it also provided an intense, euphoric sense of liberation. I didn't think about anything in particular when I ran—I just allowed myself to absorb the air as it filled my chest, rushing oxygen throughout my body, which seemed to have the amazing effect of clearing my mind and thoughts. I would see the pavement beneath my feet, hear the cars whizzing by on the road. Sometimes I ran toward a particular place, like the Grand Tree, while at others I was running just to run.

On numerous occasions, I contemplated running away and never returning to my mother ever again. I'd imagined a life free of the trappings of my personal prison, a place where I could come and go as I pleased and didn't have to report to anyone, especially someone a tyrannical as my mother. But I always went back. I think she needed me and, as crazy as it sounds, I needed her. I needed her not for what she was, but for what she was supposed to be for me. I wanted her to love me, to be proud of me, to see how smart and strong I was. I longed for her to support me and take care of me. Plus, in the back of my mind, I always thought she would change. I just knew she would come around and be that mother for me. I would soon learn that the hope that I kept in the deep recesses of my heart was a wishful longing that would never come to fruition. It became a source of pain as I realized the futility of such a craving to be loved by my mom.

At night, when nobody was around, I crawled out of my bedroom window, lied on the grass, and gazed up at the sky. The stars twinkled against the dark canvas and I wondered, *What made the stars so happy? Why did they stand out against the night sky that housed them?* It seemed like such a strange dichotomy: Here you have a darkness that blocks out the light of day, yet some stars still chose to shine.

One of these evenings in particularly stands out. The sky was clearer than any other night that I'd ever experienced. The moon was bright enough to light the ground around me, and hundreds of thousands of millions of stars lit up the sky in their collections and clusters, their galaxies and constellations.

There was one star that shined brighter than all the rest. I couldn't take my eyes off it, not even for a second. It almost felt like the star was calling me, waving a gracious hand, smiling down upon me, saying, "I see you. I see you, Darrell." Time did not exist while I was looking at this star; I don't even know how long it held my attention.

My mother's voice snapped me back into reality. From inside the house, I heard her babbling incoherently, so garbled that I couldn't make out what she was saying. As far as I could tell, she wasn't calling my name or hollering for help, so I just squatted low to the ground against the frame of the house, hoping she wouldn't come looking for me. Her rotted bedroom door hinges squeaked loudly as her door closed shut. My ears on high alert, I sat motionless, hoping she was in her room and not scouring the house for me. A few minutes passed without any babbling, yelling, or squeaking, and I knew I was safe.

Relaxed again, my eyes followed the horizon, back to the world above. I wanted to see it all, absorb every last bit of the sky. As I tilted my head upward, I sat down and rolled onto my back. With my head pressed against the grass, my arms straight at my side, my knees bent, and my feet pressed to the ground, I counted the stars. The more I counted, the more I saw. The more I saw, the more lost I felt. There were too many to count, too many to even comprehend. The universe was so vast and, at that moment, I was so small. There has to be something better out there for me. This can't be it.

As crickets chirped in the distance, I heard a soft voice. My eyes popped open and I jumped to my feet. Fists clenched and joints locked in perfect stillness, I held my breath and fixated on the voice. I looked around and nobody was there. I couldn't make out what the voice was saying or where it was coming from. Am I hallucinating? Am I crazy? Is there someone here?

No. It was just me and the Universe.

After assuring myself that everything was okay, I laid back down on the grass. As that one bright star caught my eye again, the wind brushed over me, and I heard the voice more loudly. Silently, I cried out to the Heavens, *Why God? Why me? Why do I have to be a boy here in this hell? What is this bullshit life of mine? Can't I just be one of those stars in the night sky? Please save me.* I didn't really want or expect an answer. I just wanted the Creator of the Universe to hear me.

I wanted a normal life, like the kids on TV. In the show *Leave it to Beaver*, Beaver and Wally had the perfect life: a great family, friends, a problem that could be solved in thirty minutes, and, most importantly, a mother, June Cleaver, who welcomed the boys home every night. They sat at the table and had family dinners, and I wished I would come home at night to be greeted by my mother with a big smile.

I wished I could feel her arms squeezing firmly around my body as she asked enthusiastically about my day. She would have a warm bath drawn for me and, as I cleaned up, she would be preparing the dinner table with my favorite meal: chicken and biscuits. After dinner, she would read me a bedtime story, where I could listen with wonder and amazement at the adventures of Huck and Buck. I would ask her questions like, Where are they going? Do you think they are scared? What will they do next? Will they be all right? My momma would assure me that everything was gonna be all right. But the truth was I didn't live at 211 Pine Street in Mayfield, where the grass was always green and life was always perfect. I lived at 1917 Belle

Haven Drive, where the struggle to survive was a daily ritual.

I had no idea what any of that fantasy of *Leave It to Beaver* really felt like, but seeing it on TV made me happy. It allowed for a moment of fun, a life lived vicariously through the lens of someone else, and offered me a hope that there was a better life waiting out there for me.

A silent moment passed as I wished and dreamed for this grander life, but the sound of a police siren snapped me out of the fantasy world. Then, almost as audible as the voices from the television set, I heard, "Darkness cannot exist in the presence of light. Just as a star, you are the light." I wasn't sure what that meant at the time, but I knew I would remember that moment forever.

3

RUNNING

The year was 1967. I was ten years old.

One day at school, out of nowhere—*wham*—I was knocked to the ground. My backpack sprawled open on the pavement, spilling out my notebooks and paperwork. I jumped to my feet and thought, *What the hell just happened?* Out of the corner of my right eye I saw one of the older students laughing and pointing. Trying to figure out what he could possibly want with me, I realized I left my food stamps in the front pocket of my backpack. Lunging forward, I snatched my bag off the ground before he could get to it. Those guys had a reputation for attacking the younger kids at the school and stealing their money —you either had to fight them or lose your lunch. I readied myself for the fight. I wasn't scared of these dudes, plus I had been become very familiar with an American athlete named Cassius Clay, who had just changed his name to Muhammad Ali. I recalled what I watched on the television set mere months before: Ali versus Ernie Terrell. And then there was Ali's fight from the previous year with the guy with the slick, processed hair: Cleveland Williams. All victories, all wins for the Champ. Today was my turn to be the Champ.

A small crowd of students gathered around us, formed a circle, and chanted, "Fight, fight, fight." The adrenaline in my veins exploded, sweat dripped down the back of my shirt. I stepped my left foot forward, lifted my fists to my face and, with eyes like a hawk, picked my prey.

Although outnumbered by boys much older, taller, and bigger than me, I wasn't going down without giving them everything I had. They thought it funny, a small boy with such ferocity stepping forward with so much confidence. But they had a reputation to keep, a reputation that they wouldn't allow to be dented by a little kid.

Seconds before they jumped me, the safety guards stormed the playground, breaking up the chanting circle and ushering all of us to class. I saw the dudes wave off the altercation with a laugh. One of the boys said, "Man, leave that little dude alone. That shit was funny." It wasn't my day to be Champ at the schoolyard, but I surely wasn't going to let some punk ass dudes rob me of my dignity and lunch money.

That afternoon, I noticed a place on my way home from school that I'd never seen before, even though it had been there all along: The Palmer Park Community Recreation Center. Located in Prince George's County about a mile from my house, this small red brick building soon became my second home.

The Palmer Park Recreation Center was many things to the community, but most importantly it was the boxing gym that every boy in the neighborhood wanted to join. Upon discovering the Center, I went to the gym every single day to watch and learn the intricacies of the sport.

The first time I walked in, I saw two boys in the middle of the basketball court that served as our boxing ring (the Rec Center couldn't afford a real boxing ring). The boys were much bigger than I was and clearly had years of training under their belts.

There was a man standing on the sides coaching them, telling them where to move, shouting instructions like, "Keep your hands up! Protect yourself at all times. Get your hands up!" The man then told the boys to go to opposite corners and wait for the signal to start the fight. I thought I happened upon a real live boxing match, like the ones I saw on TV, except the boys were smaller than the fighters on TV and wore protective headgear—but that's all that seemed different.

At the sound of the word, "Time," the boys danced around one another in the middle of the makeshift ring, bobbing and weaving, throwing punches and dodging the other's blows. After about a minute, the man standing on the side again hollered, "Time," to signify the end of the round. The boys stopped punching and touched gloves in a friendly way, indicating that this was not an angry fight over some wrongdoing, but rather a respectful practice session.

The man walked toward the boys, meeting them in the middle of the ring. I couldn't make out what exactly was said, but I could tell he was instructing and coaching them on ways to hold their hands, how to move to avoid punches, how to stay light on their feet. This was a sparring session, I realized, rounds of practice fights to strengthen and fine tune the skills used in real boxing matches. And the man on the side—he was the coach.

I loved every minute of being in the Rec center. Day after day, I walked home from school, anticipating my time at the gym. Whenever I watched, I thought, *Are you kidding me? They can actually hit back? I could actually hit back?* Everything in me wanted to jump in and start swinging, inviting anyone who would join me for a rowdy, angry round of punches. I saw boxing as an outlet for my anger and hurt. Outside of the ring, I could never hit back or retaliate the punches and blows that I received from my mother all these years. The frustration that came from being held hostage— the tears of my skin forming mounds of hardened tissue that covered my body and the hurt that I bottled up—was soon to come exploding out like a shaken soda can popped open by a thirsty man.

Watching the sport, I knew where I was going with boxing—all the way to the top. I not only wanted to escape my life, but I wanted to build a legacy for myself that disproved what I had heard all my life. Thanks to boxing, I would hear, "You are somebody and you matter to the world!"

It wasn't long before I made friends at the Rec center and joined the junior boxing team. Many times, I thought of my mom and the beatings that I endured and survived in order to be alive, and all I wanted to do was kill my opponent. I became the best fighter, in part as revenge for the pain that I had to endure as a helpless child.

My coach often put me with boys who were older and bigger than me. I would get whopped in the head or punched in the eye, but it didn't faze me. It wasn't shit compared to what I had felt at home. Like iron sharpening iron, the skill and intestinal fortitude to win was shaped and molded on the mat of the boxing ring at the Rec center. There, I found a peace that soothed my suffering.

Life inside of the boxing ring was much different from life outside the ring. Inside, I could control my destiny. I was the master of my fate, learning the game, perfecting the craft, and gaining mastery over my opponent. Outside the ring, I was still subjected to the fate of my genetics, unable to really control the antagonistic forces that surrounded me.

Naturally, my mother disapproved of my interest in this sport, perhaps because she knew that one day she would be stripped of her power to control me through physical and verbal abuse. She would yell and scream at me, saying that I would amount to nothing inside the ring, just like I was nothing outside the ring. Her words bounced off of me, thanks to my hardened shell, which no longer absorbed the hateful stings. I convinced myself that it didn't matter what she thought and I stayed committed to becoming a world-class fighter.

Every day before school, I snuck out of my bedroom window in the early, dark hours of the morning, ran to the park, and met my team for our morning runs. It was my brother Robert, a boy named Derrick Holmes, a boy named Ray Leonard, and Ray's brother, Roger, who we called Dale. We all came from the same neighborhood, living just doors down from one another. We'd seen each other in the streets many times before meeting at the Rec center, but we knew that in order to become one of the greatest boxing teams in the world, we would have to band together as a group of brothers. Everyone on our team took the training seriously. It was always understood that fighting was one of the few ways out of the ghetto. Sports-wise, there was no soccer program for the ghetto kids—basketball and boxing were it.

Ray and I ran behind the bus on the way to school, as the kids inside the bus screamed, "Run, catch us, run!" We knew that, in order to be World Champion, it was going to take going the extra distance, but we didn't mind the additional work.

As leader of the pack, our boxing trainer, Mr. Dave Jacobs, was there each morning. We met in the park where the Rec center was located and at the first blow of the whistle, we would take off running around the track that lined the park. Around and around we ran until our distance clocked in at five miles. It was always five miles. Nothing less would suffice.

Mr. Jacobs worked full time for the Forest Department during the day, then volunteered his afternoons and evenings to be a boxing coach. A heavyset, balding African American man, about six feet tall and 240 pounds, he wore a mustache and had hints of freckles on his medium brown skin. He had the slight look of a Creole with amazingly round, almost blinding, green eyes. I remember noticing his eyes and thinking there was just something cosmic about them; they reminded me of that star that I saw in the sky not so long ago, the one that was calling out to me.

Everyone else was scared of the morning dark, but not me: those early mornings in the park were magical compared to the darkness at home. While the other guys complained or tried to find excuses for doing their mandatory miles, I felt freer than any other time in my life. I'd tell them, "This is cool because I am out of that house." They never really asked questions about my love of running at the wee hours of the morning, so nobody knew my secrets about what went on at my house. Nobody. And after the numerous threats that I'd better not tell a soul, I locked these memories deep within the well of my being, vowing to never let the light of day reach the reality of my horrid nights.

After the five miles of roadwork, I'd run back home before my mother noticed I was gone. I'd sneak back into my room and when it was time to get ready for school, I'd run to the shower and get dressed like I'd been in my room the whole night through. As I combed my hair and brushed my teeth in the bathroom mirror, I had a slight smile across my face, knowing that I had a secret weapon in my boxing.

In order to make myself a champion, I learned to train my body as a vessel, pressing past what was comfortable. On days off from roadwork and boxing practice, I ran alone. In the weight room, I watched older boys and men lifting weights and sculpting their muscles to perfection. I watched how fast they turned the jump rope and saw their hands speeding past each other as the small speed bag bounced back and forth with each punch. As I watched their labored breathing and the sweat dripping off their brows, I said to myself, I can do that.

While training my body for optimal physical conditioning, I found myself reading more, challenging my mind to gain a greater understanding of the world and a better understanding of the human brain and body. The library at our grade school wasn't huge, but it held enough books to spark my intense love of knowledge.

The library was rather small, so small that it looked like a converted classroom. The books were arranged by subject, then categorized alphabetically by author. The lighting in the room was dim, making it difficult to see the books located high on the top shelves. We were allowed to check out two books per week, but the librarian, Mrs. Washington, grew to like me and allowed me to check out four, as long as I promised to keep my grades high. Mrs. Washington was a petite African American lady, about fifty years old. She wore black, thin-rimmed glasses and always had her hair in a tight bun on the top of her head. I often wondered if she had a family, a husband or children of her own—she seemed like a good mom.

Although the library wasn't huge, it was nonetheless overwhelming to sift through the shelves and stacks of books to find the right one. Mrs. Washington helped me navigate the library, showing me where the different sections were, how to identify author names and descriptions. One day, as I was spending my recess time in the library, she told me, "Darrell, you have something special about you. Keep reading and it will take you far in life." I never forgot those powerful words.

I made a choice to stay committed to my schoolwork and excel in spite of the social stigmas that were placed upon me by my teachers and leaders within the community. While I kept my grades high and did well academically, I still had issue relating to others on a personal level, having eradicating feelings from my life. I quickly found out that no matter how much knowledge you acquire, it doesn't erase the pain that lives deep inside of you.

Life had made me angry. I was tired of getting beaten up, being degraded, told that I would never amount to anything. As Aristotle said in *The Nicomachean Ethics*, anger at injustice is necessary to prevent further injustice. I felt righteous in my anger. I just needed a healthy outlet. Anger was going to be a great thing for boxing. After all, I'd get to beat up on somebody else and it was encouraged. (Eventually, through coaching, I learned what the Greek philosopher Seneca meant by his caveat to Aristotle's position on anger: "In sporting contests, it's a mistake to become angry.")

Whenever parents and adults at the Rec center saw me sparring or fighting, the general reaction was, "He's a loose cannon." And it was true—I was a loose cannon, just wild. When it was time to spar with my partner, my intentions were always lethal. My internal body temperature would boil and the sweat would drip down my temples. The salt-filled droplets would fall to the mat, as if in slow motion, and my world would just snap. It was cathartic for me. I felt wild and free, yet uncontrollable because all the anger and hurt would explode out from my being as I fought to stay alive each day. The thing about a loose cannon is that it's easily controlled and put back into useful space by someone who knows what they are doing, someone who can handle such a powerful weapon, someone who is an expert.

For me, that expert was my mentor, Mr. Jacobs.

There were plenty of people who said I couldn't be controlled, that the gym wasn't the place for me, who warned me to stay away. One night after boxing practice I was in the locker room and heard voices coming through the vent in the side of the wall. (When it was quiet in the locker room and you listened closely, you could hear what was being said in the room next door, the one with the PRIVATE sign glued to the door.) There were three male voices, only one of which I could identify, and that was Mr. Jacob's. I could tell by their tone that the conversation wasn't pleasant; they were obviously very upset about something. As I pressed my right ear against the slats in the vent, I heard one of them say, "That Darrell boy doesn't belong here. He is trouble." The other guy chimed in, saying, "I don't want him to be a bad influence on the team." My brow tightened as I pressed my ear harder against the vent. Mr. Jacobs then said, "He's a fine boy. He just needs a little direction. He will be alright." The two male voices blurred together as they both starting speaking at the same time.

I backed away from the vent, staring at it with disbelief. *Did they really just say that about me? They want me off the team? They don't even know me!* It took a half a second to register as I tightened my right hand into a fist, my nostrils flaring as I stood there steaming at what I just heard through the wall. I let out a roar, screaming, "Fuck you!" as I punched through the slatted vent that had just been the conduit for the three voices on the other side of the wall. As I threw my gloves and boxing gear into my duffle bag and slung it across my shoulder, Mr. Jacobs came running through the locker room door. His stance was firm, his arms outstretched, palms facing upward, a look of concern on his face. "What's the matter, Darrell?"

I said nothing.

I ran out of the gym that day feeling overwhelmed by the doubt cast my way by people who didn't even know me. I never found out who those other two men were, but it really didn't matter to me. Whoever they were, I was determined to prove them dead wrong. Becoming a skilled Warrior and learning to fight back would not only be freedom from my bondage, it would eventually lead me to my greater calling.

4

MENTORING THE MADNESS

I'd just completed one of the best boxing practices of my life.

My punches were flying effortlessly. I was fast with my hands, light on my feet, and was finally gaining an understanding of what it meant to make my opponent miss. I had practiced for months, and the repetitive training, day in and day out, was solidifying a sense of precision and excellence. I was becoming a bona fide fighter.

We had a rapid-fire punch drill that we did everyday with Mr. Jacobs, a drill designed to sharpen our quickness and condition our hands to fly on instinct. Mr. Jacobs would hold up his padded hands and call out a series of punches—One. One, Two. One, Two. One, Two, Three—and we had to respond within milliseconds in order to avoid getting hit with his padded gloves. After my rapid-fire punch drill, Mr. Jacobs looked at me and said with a big grin, "That's what I'm talking about." I smiled back. I had nailed every single one of the punch combinations without hesitation, like a pro. He walked towards me and firmly patted me on the back, saying "I'm proud of you son." Instinctively, I arched my back and lunged forward as I clenched my teeth in pain.

Before Mr. Jacobs could question my spastic movement, I called out to Ray Leonard, "Yo man, let me holla at you," and quickly walked away. I could see Mr. Jacobs in my peripheral view carefully watching me walk away. His brows crunched together, and I'm sure his mind was racing with confusion. I suspect he realized that his firm pat on my back brought intense pain, and he wondered why I hadn't said anything to him earlier about being hurt. He never asked me about it, but he also never touched me on my back again.

The next day after practice, Mr. Jacobs walked up to me and asked, "Would you like to join me and my family for dinner tonight?"

"I have to get home," I said, and then immediately left. As I walked toward my apartment house, I wondered what the Jacobs family would be eating for dinner. I knew my dinner was going to be something mixed with government cheese, or some more fried chicken. I was sure whatever ended up on the Jacobs' dinner table would be much tastier than that.

The next day, he asked again. I told him that I could come over on Saturday because I was always out of the house on the weekends, so my mother wouldn't question my whereabouts. He gave me a huge grin and said, "Okay, then. Be at my house at 3:00 PM."

"Okay," I said, "see you then." Admittedly, I was hesitant to accept the offer. I just didn't know what to expect. It wasn't that I was scared to have dinner somewhere, because I had eaten dinner plenty of times at other people's houses. There was just something different about Mr. Jacobs, almost like he knew things about me even though I'd never shared them with anyone else in the world, much less with him.

The following Saturday, I arrived on his doorstep at 3:00 PM on the dot. After I walked into the house, I was greeted with a hug from Mrs. Jacobs. I heard children playing in the distance, and the house was filled with laughter and love. As I slowly made my way through the living room, I caught a glimpse of the TV, ran my fingers across the soft fabric of the sofa, then turned the corner into the clean, polished kitchen. My senses were overwhelmed with the smell of freshly cooked meatloaf and vegetables. I fumbled with my hands and shifted my weight from one foot to the other in anticipation of a glorious meal.

When we sat down for dinner, I wanted to attack the food, but I wasn't sure what to do with all of the forks and knives. I wondered who all the extra silverware was for—surely all those weren't for one person. Meals at my house were usually eaten with our hands – fried chicken, biscuits, cheese or peanut butter sandwiches. The dinnerware, the silverware, the napkins, the glasses, the subtle candle glowing in the middle of the table, made this moment surreal. There wasn't too much conversation at the table, but the energy of the room was nice, comforting. Mrs. Jacobs asked me about my interests—aside from boxing, of course. I kept my answers short and to the point, but I don't think she minded. Mr. Jacobs and his family gave me a glimpse into happiness that I may have never known had it not been for his influence in my life.

With his pleasant, uplifting nature, Mr. Jacobs always gave me the feeling that things were going to be all right. I often wished I had a dad like him. He was a symbol of hope that there was something still good in the world. With his soft, father-like voice, he encouraged me to always be truthful and work hard. I loved that whenever I'd nail a combination, he'd say, "There you go," with a smile and a nod. He was a beacon of light in my dark world.

With the patience of my coach and my persistence to be the best fighter in the world, I began to excel in boxing. Months after sparring and training, I entered my first official boxing match. Our team was fighting in a tournament in D.C., and I was set to challenge a junior amateur from the other side of the tracks. I couldn't wait to jump into the ring. I kept asking Mr. Jacobs, "Is it my turn yet?"

Finally he nodded and said, "Darrell, you up."

I bounded from my seat and ran up the stairs into the boxing ring. Mr. Jacobs was giving me some last minute reminders and handed me a piece of chocolate (He always gave us a piece of chocolate before our fights – he believed it gave us energy). As I took the candy, I nodded my head at his advice, but heard none of what he said. But I knew what I had to do: trust my training. I moved back into my corner and, within seconds, the bell rang and the battle was on.

My opponent and I met in the middle of the ring. He had a look of slight confusion on his face, like he was asking himself if this was a real fight or not. Oh, it was definitely real. The blur of the noise, the hum of the air conditioner fans blowing above our heads, the voices of the coaches in the corners, the screams from teammates, parents, and fans in attendance: all collided into a sweet song of bliss. Just as a conductor brings together the instrumentalists in his orchestra, the chaos of the world swayed in perfect unity. It was like a supernatural force took over me in the ring. I had felt glimpses of this surge of power in my sparring sessions, but nothing had overwhelmed me quite like this.

The punches were so natural, so organic, so real. I hit that kid with at least twenty punches in the first minute of the round. He caught me once on the chin, but I don't remember feeling it at all—I didn't know I'd been hit until somebody mentioned it to me after the fight was done.

The ref stepped between us and asked him if he was okay. I stood back, peeking around the ref, wanting to see my opponent, to see what was going on. I guess the kid said no, that he wasn't okay, because the ref waved his hands in the air, signaling the end of the fight. That was it. I was victorious in my first official bout. I looked around to find Mr. Jacobs and he was clapping enthusiastically and said to me, "Great job!" I raised my hands in victory and climbed out of the ring, eagerly anticipating my next battle.

Fighting in tournaments and winning trophies soon became the norm, but the prizes and trophies didn't really mean much to me because, other than Mr. Jacobs, there wasn't a soul in the crowd who cared whether I left the ring victoriously or if I died on the mat.

As I got stronger, leaner, and faster, the fights grew fiercer. My pain and rage swelled within me as the battle unfolded on the mat. I got angrier and more destructive as time wore on. When that bell rang to start the fight, I snapped into a lethal, unconscious, walking coma. Nothing short of killing the man on the other side was good enough for me. My vicious attacks were nothing personal against my opponent, but rather an all-out lashing against all the injustice and abuse I'd suffered. After my fights, my teammates and people in the crowd would say things like, "You look like the devil himself inside that ring." Bloodshot eyes and an unrelenting rage turned me into a demon, a demon who wasn't afraid to get punched. Pain in the ring meant nothing to me—with the wounds inflicted by my mother, I was used to it.

I held deep-rooted rage that exploded uncontrollably in the ring, and Mr. Jacobs taught me what the ancient philosopher Seneca meant: I had to learn how to channel my pain and frustration into something that would turn up positive for me. I was always reminded to relax, to breathe, and to not get angry in the ring. It was about precision and understanding the movements and reactions of the human body. Boxing is the art of a sweet science, one that I was committed to master.

It was a warm Sunday morning in 1968, and as the sun crept up the horizon, the rays of light beamed through my shadeless window, waking me with a reminder that another fearful night had passed.

Sundays weren't the best day of the week for me.

It started out like any other Sunday morning. For me, going to church was much more of a ritual than a spiritual experience, but that wasn't the case for the rest of my family—they were all up in the Holy Ghost, so we went to church religiously. Church was seen as the Sanctuary for black folks, a place of identity for people who believed. The United House of Prayer provided not just a place of gathering for like-minded people, but it offered an experience. At the front of the church was a full band, complete with an organ, guitars, drums, and a full choir, which, at the time, seemed like a rock band to me. There were always people shouting and screaming and dancing up and down the aisles, and I'd sit wide-eyed, watching the fat ladies rolling down the aisle, speaking in tongues. Even though it wasn't a spiritual experience, it was a place of peace because everyone was on their best behavior; all the dysfunction was hidden as the goody two-shoe front was proudly put forward. I knew I wouldn't get beat at church, so there was some comfort for me at the United House of Prayer.

This particular Sunday morning, as the church service rolled on, just outside the walls of the church building, civil unrest mounted as civilians rioted, running the streets, breaking windows, looting and robbing. Just around the corner sirens bellowed and screams filled the city streets. Little did we know that something bigger was lurking on the outside. A heavy cloud of unrest was erupting throughout the world.

The charismatic uproar of the church service did little to interest me in the matters of religion or life beyond this Earth. All I knew was that the people inside the four walls of the chapel were not the same people behind the doors of their own homes. I had that much figured out. But church did have something worthwhile for me: at the end of the service they served fried chicken in the basement. That was some of the best fried chicken that I ever ate.

This Sunday went down as the best and the worst day at church I ever had. Sprinting from the service and down into the basement, I picked up the fried chicken dinner and rushed back up the stairs to meet my mother and brother at the car. Bursting through the door of the church, my sprint slowed to a walk as I notice five huge, red fire trucks lining the road in front of the church. I stared at the firemen as they dutifully assembled their hoses and readied themselves for extinguishing. My pulse raced, and I flashed on an engulfed building standing right behind me. I snapped my head around, expecting to see orange flames roaring through the roof, people running and screaming in fear, smoke billowing up from the ground but I saw none of that. Nothing. No fire, no smoke, no fear. Not yet.

As I turned my gaze back towards the fire truck, I realized it wasn't a building that was on fire, but rather people. *Was this the end times? Was Jesus coming back? Why were these people on fire?* I had to know what exactly was going on, so I ran towards the action, calling after my brother, "Come see!"

Rushing up to the crowd of soaked patrons, I realize there was no fire. The people were soaked, running from the hoses, covering their children and screaming in fear. Nobody was on fire, so I wondered, *What's with the water?*

My brother grabbed my shoulder and said, "Come on! We gotta get out of here! They're gonna spray us too!" I didn't know what was causing the water party, but I was determined to be involved. I could hear my mother's firm voice in the distance: "Get back here, boys! Come on, let's go." I sensed the fear in her voice and saw the angst in the faces of the people getting sprayed, yet felt nothing but excitement.

I rushed out into the water, yelling "Woo-hoo!" as my brother chased after me. The freedom of slipping up and down the water soaked streets of DC in our Sunday suits, the suits that were never supposed to get dirty, seemed like the most magical moment in my life.

My brother screamed, "Don't do it! Don't get wet! We have to go! Come on Darrell," but I didn't stop. I enjoyed the total freedom of running, all the while making sure to keep a firm grip on the chicken dinner, clueless that the men pointing their hoses into the faces of innocent bystanders didn't mean it as a generous outpouring of cool water on a hot summer Sunday. Instead, it was the mark of discrimination and injustice at a people who were simply fighting for their own rights.

Chaotic, riotous conditions had popped up seemingly overnight. DC was a powder keg of civil unrest, similar to the simmering anger that flowed through the country after the assassination of Martin Luther King, Jr. As we exited the church, we walked into a battlefield that dwarfed the problems within our own lives.

As a product of the civil rights era, I soon realized that the unrest through the city of DC meant terror for citizens whose skin was a bit darker. But as a child whose unrest, war, and terror lived inside the walls of my home, there was nothing outside on the streets that could possibly scare me.

Eventually it became commonplace to see the National Guard lining the roads, holding machine guns, siccing dogs at the crowds of protestors, spraying water and mace, beatings and pummeling whatever stood in their way. But I would soon learn the magnitude of such hate and discrimination.

The year was 1969. I was twelve years old.

"Great fight."

That's what Mr. Jacobs told me as I triumphantly stepped out of the ring on the night of July 11, 1969. Throwing blow after blow on the war-laden mat of the boxing ring, I had earned the biggest trophy of my career. My team— Robert, Ray, Dale, and Derrick—greeted me with glorious praise, saying, "Yes! Great job Darrell! You did it. That was awesome!" After dominating my opponent, further securing my place in the world of boxing, I felt like a King.

Mr. Jacobs drove me home, and I proudly held my trophy in my lap. The trophy—my gold, towering symbol of perfection—reached just above my head. I had to crane my chin and eyes in order see the perfectly poised gold boxer on top. This trophy felt different from all of the others ones. It was by far the biggest, so maybe it was its towering height that excited me.

Approaching the front door of my apartment, I saw the screen door had been left open, an unmistakable sign that my mother was home. I slowly opened the door and saw her lying asleep on the living room sofa. I quietly tip- toed to my bedroom, careful not to wake her. Exhausted from the fight, I fell into my bed and was asleep in seconds.

Around 2:00 I was jolted out of my slumber by the sound of my mother stomping down the hallway. She flung open my door. When she turned on the light, dozens of roaches frantically ran to find shelter. She walked over to my bed, pulled my head up by my left ear, and yelled, "Sit up straight on the goddamn bed, because I have something to show you."

Sitting up straight on the goddamn bed, I blinked my eyes hard, trying to adjust to the sudden light. Out from behind her back, she revealed a hammer. Slowly stepping towards me, she stared me in the face and said, "You ain't shit, and that damn trophy don't mean shit to nobody."

Without taking her cold dark eyes from mine, she grabbed the top of the trophy and slowly slid it across the bedroom floor, positioning it directly in front of me. My stomach dropped when she said, "If you move one inch,

I will bust this hammer over your goddamn head, you hear me?" She gripped the hammer by the black rubber handle with both hands, her right hand positioned directly above her left, her brown knuckles turning white from her clamp-like grip.

Before I could even say, "Don't," she raised the hammer high above her head and, with every ounce of her strength, arched her back and slammed it down onto the five-foot trophy, crushing it into millions of pieces. As the fragments of gold plastic flew around the room, my jaw clenched tight, and my eyes fixed forward. I knew if I moved one inch, my head would be the next thing to get slammed.

She spit on the trophy pieces, turned, and walked out of the room. Devastated, I stared at the trophy shards. Raw anger welled up inside of my chest, begging to be released, but I couldn't scream, so the blood in my body boiled, and sweat dripped down the side of my face. Just as tears run down the face of those who are sad, sweat from anger runs down my brow. I don't get sad. I get mad.

When I was sure the Monster was gone, I jumped onto the floor, went to my knees, and frantically tried to gather all the pieces. With the hurt overwhelming my mind, soul, and body, I cupped my hands and made sweeping movements across the linoleum, shuffling the broken bits into piles. Maybe I can put it back together, I thought, but soon realized that would be futile. The piles were rubbish, ready to be vacuumed up and thrown in the trash.

This wasn't the first trophy she'd broken, but this time she crushed not only the trophy, but my spirit. I felt that no matter what I achieved, no matter how big my prizes were, it would never be good enough for her. As I looked at the pieces scattered about on the floor, I realized that my options were limited. Everything in me wanted revenge and it seemed the only satisfaction that I would ever have would be to eliminate her from my life—permanently.

The year was 1970. I was thirteen years old.

I felt so alone in the world. Yes, I had my friends, my boxing team, and Mr. Jacobs, but they all felt so distant. I was hiding the truth, I had to suppress my real thoughts and feelings and keep the truth bottled inside, pressed way down into the depths. The pain strangled me and forced me to lash out in anger and destruction. I wanted to feel something, anything, so I turned to rage to remind me that I was still alive.

When I was at my lowest points, I would wonder, *Where's my father? Why did he leave me, why did he abandon me? Does he know that I suffer at the Monster's hands each night? Does he care that I was abused and felt lost?* Since I don't have a good mom, couldn't I at least have a dad who cared? I would make up stories about how my other brothers and sisters would one day reunite and play games and talk about sports and have family reunions. However, all of this was simply fantasy—the truth was, he wasn't there, and would likely never be there. It was just me against my mother. But I dared not ask my mother about him for fear of severe retaliation.

But, out of nowhere, my father appeared on my thirteenth birthday—October 8, 1970—and when he showed up, it was magical.

He'd called my mother several days before and told her that he wanted to pick me up and spend the day with me. I didn't hear the conversation, but knowing my mother, I'm certain it came with some stipulations about what we could and couldn't do together. Her need to control everything was unrelenting.

Even though she took the call early in the day, she waited until nightfall to tell me the news. She found me in my bedroom, reading a book from the school library, when she burst through the door and said, "You're going with your pops tomorrow." I looked up from the book, confused, but before I could ask anything, she said, "No questions. Just be ready to go around five," then turned and stomped out of the room.

I smacked the book closed and sat up. I didn't really know what to think or how to react. Confusion surfaced as all of my questions about this man came rushing forward in my mind. I'm still not sure why my mother allowed me to go with him.

My birthday afternoon couldn't come soon enough. A couple hours before my dad's scheduled arrival, I dressed in my finest clothes: a pair of black slacks, shiny black patent leather shoes, a white button down shirt with a plaid bow tie. I stood at the bathroom mirror, making sure my hair looked perfect, and coughing as I sprayed much too much cologne on my body. I wanted my pops to be proud of me, to see what a handsome young man I had become. I felt like this day would be the start of a wonderful relationship, one that would carry on for years to come.

I was ready to go at 5:00. But 5:00 came and went. So did 5:30. I began to get worried that this was a cruel joke that my mother played on me. Thinking that maybe my dad was out in the driveway waiting for me, I got up and walked to the door—nothing. Just as I turned to walk back to the sofa, my eyes widened as a pristine, black 1965 Ford Mustang rolled silkily into our driveway, and out came my father.

He looked like someone from the movies and I thought, *That's my dad?* He was a handsome man, about 5'8", slender, probably weighing in around one hundred seventy pounds. He had smooth skin, unblemished by time. It was hard to tell how old he was.

He walked from his car to the porch with his hands in his pockets. He nodded towards my mother and asked, "How y'all doin'?" He spoke to my mother as if she were a stranger, but that shouldn't have been a surprise, as the didn't have much to talk about.

She apathetically said, "Good." Then, turning towards me, she said, "Go on with your pops, Darrell."

I just stood and stared at him silently—hell, I didn't know what to say. He took his hands from his pants pockets, put his right arm around my shoulder, looked down to me, and said, "All right, son. You ready? We are going to the drive-in theatre."

A conflicting, massive rush of emotions flooded me as I tried to process that. Son? He called me son. Son. Yes, I'm his son and that's my pops. And did he just say the *drive-in?* A real live picture show? I thought this may be what kids feel at Christmas, when all of their wishes come true. I had seen plenty of movies on the black and white television at our house or at friend's houses but I'd only ever heard about the drive-in movie theatre, and had certainly never been to one.

We walked out the front door and down the steps of the apartment and towards the car. I spotted my reflection in the car as I slowly walked toward the passenger side door—fresh wax on black was like a mirror to the rest of the world. My father took the lead and walked to the right side of the car. He opened the door for me and with a big smile said, "Jump in."

The sun was low in the sky as dusk was quickly approaching. The evening twilight was cool and the scent of the car seats filled my nose, smelling like brand new leather boots, fresh out the factory. Buckled in on the passenger side, staring straight ahead, I cut my eyes left to see my father out of the corner of my eye. After he fidgeted with the controls on the door of the driver side for a bit, he said, "Let me know if you're comfortable."

Comfortable? It was beyond comfort. It was luxury and intense pleasure. As I ran my hands over the leather seats, I felt the firmness, almost like this seat had never been sat in. He was holding it just for me. The song on the radio was "So I Can Love You," by the Emotions. It wasn't loud or overwhelming, it softly filled the car like a mothers voice whispering a lullaby to her baby. I smiled, took a deep breath, and replied, "I'm fine."

We arrived at the theater about fifteen minutes later. The sight of the cars, the laughter of the people, the coolness of the night, it all evoked a sense of happiness that I'd never before experienced. I had no idea what movie we would see or how this would all work out—I just knew it was much different from what I was used to. And I loved it.

My father chose *The Ten Commandments*, starring Charleston Heston as Moses. To a child who had only been exposed to black and white television, seeing the screen fill up with elaborate spectacle was overwhelming. This movie was unlike anything that I had ever seen: the colors, the music, the people, the message. It was speaking directly to me. The voices of the actors penetrated the window of the car and I found myself gazing into the eyes of Moses, my mouth gaping open as I hinged on every word.

I knew of Moses and his message from Sunday school. I knew that he was found as a baby in a basket, raised by a family not his own, endured hardships and trials, and was ultimately chosen to deliver God's people. I knew the story, but that night the story came alive.

After seeing this movie, I was never the same. I thought, So, this was the God that I had heard so much about, the One who could deliver people from bondage, perform wondrous signs and miracles and save people. There was a line from the movie that filled my nights with lovely dreams: from a burning bush, God told Moses, "Put off thy shoes, for thou art on Holy Ground." While many would have been scared on account of the fire, my love intensified as the words of God continued to penetrate my soul. For days and weeks after seeing the movie, I looked for signs that God was talking to me. Not only did the movie further spark my passionate curiosity about my larger purpose in this world, but also lit a fire within for all things cinematic. My love of movies, their power to bring me directly into the reality of the film, would strengthen with each movie that I was privileged to see throughout my lifetime.

While I had hoped this would be one of many experiences with my father, it was one of the few times that we spent together, but I was eternally grateful for each moment with him. I believe our meetings were divinely orchestrated in order that I be exposed to my greater calling and be prepared for what the Universe had planned for me.

The next day, I went over to Cozy's apartment to tell him about meeting my Father, and how *The Ten Commandments* so changed me. But when I walked into the apartment, Cozy and Derrick were rolling dice. I asked them what they were doing and Derrick said, "Tryin to figure out whose car we goin' to steal."

They laughed and I looked at them like they were crazy. I asked, "Why y'all want to steal a car?"

"We just wanna go joy ridin, that's all," Derrick said.

I said, "Let my roll determine which car." I rolled the white dice around in my hands, feeling the four sides rub against my palms. I cupped my hands together and blew a warm puff of air into my hands, shook them up and down and let the dice fly onto the floor. We watched as they rolled end over end and landed on the side with the six black dots.

"Alright, it's the blue Impala down the way. Let's go," Derrick yelled.

We went outside and sprinted towards the car, chatting about our imminent joy ride down the strip of Palmer Park. When we made it to the Impala, we strolled over to the driver side of the car, where Cozy yanked on the handle. It didn't budge. It was locked.

We hadn't thought about that.

Derrick went around the back of the car, looking through the piles of junk in the garage for something he could use to pop the lock. Cozy yelled out, "Get a screwdriver."

I walked back toward Cozy's place to look for a screwdriver, but before I could reach the back of the car, Derrick called out, "Found one!" Derrick handed the screwdriver to Cozy and, being the clever, mischievous boy that he was, he quickly popped the lock. Nice! It was about to be on and poppin'. We all jumped into the baby blue coupe, ready to get our drive on through downtown. But we must have made a little too much commotion because before we could think about how to get the car started, the man inside the house rushed towards us, screaming and waving around some kind of weapon.

"Oh, shit!" I hollered. "We gotta get out of here."

Derrick yelled, "Go, go, go! Get out the side door—go!" When Cozy got the door open, Derrick pushed him out of the car and he fell down onto the gravel driveway. I jumped over them and took off running. When I looked back, they were both behind me—as was the man from the house, wearing only a pair of boxer shorts and screaming, "You muthafuckin' kids!"

It paid off to be the hardest working fighters on the boxing team, because at that moment, all of those miles sure came in handy. We ran as fast and as far as we could to get away from that crazy man with the knife, or gun, or whatever the hell he had in his hand.

When we finally made it back to Cozy's apartment, we burst into laughter. Once I regained control of myself, "Man, y'all crazy." Derrick, still trying to catch his breath, said, "Darrell, you was about to leave Cozy as the sacrificial lamb."

I laughed and said, "Shit, I wasn't goin' down for y'alls crazy asses."

We never tried to steal a car again—or at least not with the owner right inside the house. And I never did get the chance to tell them about what happened with my father. And I sure wish I had.

5

ANGER WILL DESTROY YOU

The year was 1973. I was sixteen years old.

Six years into my boxing training, I competed in the most prestigious competition in the world of amateur boxing, the Golden Gloves, where boxing teams from around the country met annually to determine the best of the best. Through a series of fights, one winner becomes the titleholder for the Golden Gloves for that year. Many Golden Gloves titleholders go on to become professional fighters: among them, greats like Joe Louis, Muhammad Ali, and Sugar Ray Leonard.

In 1973, the Golden Gloves champion was Darrell Foster.

I hoped winning the Golden Gloves would make my momma proud—after all, it did mean that I was the best. I received congratulations from my friends, my teammates, my coach, and even random people who had just heard of my winning. It gave me confidence and bravado and only strengthened the chip I had on my shoulder. While I was proud of my accomplishment and the esteem that I received for winning, I found no congratulations or satisfaction from the one person that I desperately wanted to see me.

And when I took home the trophy, there was no family there to congratulate me.

My coach—who may as well have been family—mentored me to greatness inside the ring. But the one thing Mr. Jacobs couldn't control was the rage on the inside of my soul. Even though he never asked me about my personal life, I always had a feeling that he somehow just knew. I wasn't the only troubled kid that he coached in his career, and he had a way of connecting and reading between the lines and being able to reach out and touch those parts of your life that would push you to greater achievements. As a man of few words, much of his coaching was done through actions, something that stuck with me throughout my whole life.

My next fight, the fight after the Golden Gloves, proved to be my last in the ring with this team. It started like any other fight, but midway through the bout, I felt the blood vessels in my eyes start to swell, making my eyes appear completely bloodshot (This is why I sometimes looked like the devil in the ring). My heart thumped hard against my chest. My nostrils flared as I inhaled and exhaled deep red breaths of revenge. Not revenge against anything that my opponent did, but revenge for all of the beatings I'd endured. This guy on the other side of the ring could never have imagined what was about to hit him.

In a flash of anger, I saw my mother's face on this guy's body. So clear, so vivid, so enraging. Charging toward my opponent, I unloaded a six-punch combination to the right side of his face. As he moved to block his head with his hands, I took advantage of his open body and unloaded another seven-punch combination to his left side. Toppling over in pain, he hit the mat. But I would not stop. All I could hear through the noise of the crowd were the words of my mother—"You ain't shit and ain't never gonna be shit!"—and in that moment, that kid was her.

The referee tried to get between us, but I was unrelenting. The guy was pinned to the floor on his back, my body on top of him, my arms swinging with every ounce of power and force that I had. I felt no pain. I felt no exhaustion. I actually felt *peace*.

The referee, my team, and the entire crowd saw me beating the living shit out of a random stranger, but they had no idea that the reason I would not stop was that I was exacting my revenge. Finally, when the ref blew the whistle and the bell rang, more than one person in the crowd yelled, "Stop! Stop! You are going to kill him." Mr. Jacobs also screamed, "Let him go! The round is over!"

Enraged, I couldn't stop. I kept pounding him until his body was splattered with blood, and his eyes were swollen shut from the impact of hundreds of vengeful punches. Finally, with the assistance of two other men, the referee pulled me off of the poor kid and threw me into my corner. Mr. Jacobs jumped into the ring, shoving me back against the ropes, holding my arms down, and as calmly as he could, he told me to "Relax. Relax. Relax."

He'd seen me in a fury many times before, when sparring practice got more heated than a friendly training regimen should, but here I remained in a manic state, yelling like a ferocious lion, angry that my prey had been spared. A few deep breaths later, I realized what just happened. Angry at the situation, angry at myself, I jerked my arms free and jumped out of the ring, and trudged heavy- footed to the locker room.

The locker room was full of other fighters and their coaches, preparing for their bouts in the tournament. As I walked past an open locker, I punched the locker door so hard that the bottom hinge broke off, leaving the metal locker door swinging back and forth as the room hushed to a deafening silence.

I ripped off my gloves and plopped hard onto the beach in the middle of the locker room. Replaying the fight and the hurt look in Mr. Jacobs' eyes was heart-wrenching. He was not only furious at my behavior, but he was supremely disappointed. I wasn't only representing myself in the ring; I represented him, my team, my community, and because I lost control, I was stripped of my Golden Gloves title and disqualified from boxing. There are no records of my winnings, there are no records of my disqualifications. I was erased from the system. I simply never existed. The days and weeks after my disqualification and exile from the sport that I loved, I began to wonder if the Monster was right. Were my mother's words taking over my life? Why am I in bondage to the lies?

Anger took it away from me that night. Boxing was supposed to be my way out of the ghetto—shit, it was *anyone-who-could-throw-a-punch's* way out of the ghetto. We had to fight. Unfortunately, there were no second chances. As talented as I was and as skilled as I had become, Mr. Jacobs' prophecy came true: "You can't get angry in the ring. It will destroy you."

6

ON MY OWN

My situation at home never improved, and, after much deliberation on how to get rid of the Monster, I decided to be the bigger person and leave, vowing to never look back.

I rose above the pain and stood taller than her, always pressing, always studying, and always training in order to get the hell out of that town. Besides, if I killed my mother, she'd win, and that was one thing I couldn't live with. I had to be the better person. I couldn't go out as a no-good, you-ain't-shit inmate, because my worst nightmare of her being right would come true.

The problem was that I had no family in Maryland, nobody to run to. I hadn't seen my father in years and wasn't about to go looking for him. In fact, ever since I found out that he was the junkman at ABC Junk Yard—where Cozy and I used to go steal things—I lost some of my warm feelings. Besides, he couldn't have given me what I wanted, which was freedom.

Yes, I had friends—Cozy, Ray, Derrick—but the life of the ghetto was tough: every man for himself. Occasionally I slept at a friend's house, but most nights I found myself sleeping on top of dryers at the laundromat, their front doors protected by the drug addicts who stood watch. The laundromat was closed and locked for the night, in an effort to keep the bums out. But I always found a way to get inside. Each night, I climbed onto an industrial sized dryer, my safe place from the world, and slipped into the world of dreams as the dryer hummed, rocked, and warmed my body to sleep.

The addicts protected me because I would steal a wallet and give it to them without asking for anything in return other than a roll of dimes. The Laundromat dryers would run all night on a roll of dimes, so dimes were all I needed to stay warm. They were really cool with me, these junkies, because the money from the stolen wallet allowed them to cop their fix for the night, which was why they gladly gave me my dimes and guarded the laundromat entrance.

Once I left home, I never went back. I had to keep it moving. I didn't have an elaborate plan on how I would survive on the streets. I just knew I'd figure it out somehow, some way.

Despite having no place to call home, I made sure I had a place in the world. Through my deliberate studies and ambitious of leadership, I became Student Body President of Largo High School and achieved top ranked leadership of my ROTC. Although I was no longer officially part of the boxing team, I understood the importance of training to keep performing at a world class level in every aspect of my life. I continued to train and box to keep my mind sharp and my body a finely tuned machine. I still prepared for a fight, but not a fight that would take place inside a ring.

In addition to school and boxing, I held an all-night job at the U.S. Post Office. Around the time I was hired there was a USPS strike that caused chaos for the post office, and, as a result, they began to hire clerk casuals to load trucks at their bulk mail centers. They were looking for anyone who could sling packs of mail and parcel packages, particularly young, buff dudes who could handle the physical labor. That was me.

I was assigned the worst possible shift: 6:00 PM to 2:00 AM. Mail from all over the world—envelopes, packages, boxes, gifts—poured down the conveyor belts faster than I could get my hands on. I was finishing up my senior year in high school, earning money through the post office job to pay rent at friends' houses (I was never the loner type). I didn't want handouts or to mooch off of anyone else. I wanted to earn my stay and pay for my room and board.

The job allowed me to make money, feed myself, and take care of my needs. During the weeks leading up to Christmas, it also showed me how much people loved each other—I never realized folks got so many gifts, and had so many who cared about them. Toys, trucks, games, clothes, money—if you can name it, it was coming through the mail, and my hands were the ones spreading the holiday love across the country.

I realized that my dreams, my destiny, my path out of the trenches, wouldn't come through boxing. That institution had rejected me, so I had to find another way out.

Reading fascinated me. I had always heard of people having stories read to them as children. Since I didn't have that experience, I read to myself, and I decided I would conquer the world of business. I may have had unfortunate circumstances, but I was determined to succeed, no matter what the odds. I always managed to find time for the library, reading as many texts, novels, screenplays, biographies, autobiographies of leaders of the world, as I could get my hands on. If I were nowhere to be found, I was often at one of the numerous public libraries in D.C. or else at the library at the University of Maryland.

Although my love of books, stories, and knowledge empowered me, I knew the importance of physicality when it came to achieving the things that I wanted to have in my life, so I put in grueling hours of work in order to stay physically fit. I made it a habit to get up at 6:00 AM and run five miles, no matter what. Even though I was no longer on a boxing team, I trained like I was. I often met my old teammates for roadwork in the mornings and worked out with them in the gym in the afternoons.

It was at this point that I knew my life was destined for greatness. I figured that if I survived those first sixteen years, I could survive and conquer anything. Life had molded me for struggle. My demons raged inside of me and there were times that I thought about returning just to get revenge on my mother, but I knew I had to choose the higher road, because if I abused her, I'd become her.

I made a vow that I would leave Maryland and move to the West Coast to get as far away as possible from any and every thing that reminded me of my upbringing. Having a successful business and becoming a leader to other people in the world was where I had my sights set. This is how I would win my fight—and I knew what I needed to do to get there.

All throughout high school, I made a deliberate effort to keep my grades up, knowing that I would be dropped from my ROTC leadership role if I failed to keep my commitment to academic excellence. I knew if college were a dream ever to be realized, than a full scholarship was the only way I would see it come to fruition. While there were many times that I was tempted to release my responsibility from ROTC, the lure of a full paid

scholarship to the University of Maryland kept me in line.
So, the next stop: The University of Maryland.

7

THE PARADOX

The year was 1974. I was seventeen years old.

The University of Maryland campus is located in College Park, Maryland, just outside of Washington, D.C. I had experience with the University long before I was old enough to attend. The rough lifestyle of the ghetto often led me to the campus seeking goods and substances that I knew would turn into cash. Drugs were commonplace in the ghetto. Anything that would help soothe the harsh pain of reality—the hunger, the depression, the feeling of nothingness, lost dreams, dashed hopes, and the cruelty of life inside the walls of a caged existence—was welcomed with open arms. You did what you had to do to survive.

Having received a full scholarship to the University of Maryland through my involvement in the ROTC at Largo High School, I was admitted into IED, the early acceptance program at the University. Emancipated minors received room and board for their first year, so, just like that, I had a place of my own.

I soon met Stan Jackson, who would turn into one of my lifelong friends. Stan was a couple of years my senior and was known for his flamboyant style and impressive dress. But Stan didn't have anything on me: I would always come to campus dressed to the nines. Everyone was impressed. Folks thought they were the best dressed until I came along. My tailored suits, pristine shoes, crisp shirts, sharp ties, and carved-out physique made me quite popular, quite fast.

How could I afford all of this? Turned out that money wasn't a problem: my job at the post office, my dealings on the side, and my late night efforts to earn extra cash were paying for my expensive clothes and fine sports car. In the late hours of the night, I visited the slums of the ghetto, where the junkies were paying young dudes money to shoot them in the neck with cocaine-filled needles. The holes, scars, and thick tissue that covered these junkie's arms from years of shooting up prevented them from a cocaine buzz that would get them through the night. They trusted the young boys to come by and, with their good eyesight, hit a vein in their neck, flooding their bloodstream with the new euphoric reality. (Although I was around a lot of drugs, I never got caught up in them myself. I was, however, torn—I understood the allure of numbing a lifetime of disappointment and pain, so I passed no judgment on the users, but at the same time I realized that being a victim to another idol, the drugs, was not the life I wanted for myself.)

Even before school started, people around campus knew about me. At parties with my new friends and acquaintances, strangers would walk up to me and say, "You Darrell Foster, huh? I heard about you." Depending on who you asked, I was either the best or the worst person to know. I guess it depended on if you were on my good side or bad side.

Though I came from the streets, I realized I had to be a bigger man if I was going to move forward, and that meant controlling my temper. As time passed, my anger and revenge for all my hurts and pains would soon become an outward expression of intense violence even as I tried to keep focused on the bigger plan of success. Fights and physical altercations became the norm for me. Although I never went out looking for a fight, the fight seemed to always find a way of seeking me out and finding me.

I was dependent upon nobody for my survival, but was drawn to a group of people who belonged to the Omega Psi Phi fraternity. Founded on November 17, 1911 at Howard University in Washington, D.C., Omega Psi Phi Fraternity, Inc. was the first international fraternal organization on the campus of a historically black college. The name Omega Psi Phi comes from the initials of the Greek phrase meaning, "Friendship is Essential to the Soul," which is also the motto for the organization. Central to the fraternity are the principles of Manhood, Scholarship, Perseverance, and

Uplift. The men I met during my time at Maryland became not only friends for life, but my family, my brothers. All members of the frat—especially Stan Jackson, Sam Northington, and Jose Flora—formed a brotherly bond that continues to remain strong and steadfast to this day.

Gaining entrance into the fraternity was no easy feat. Unlike honorary members, to gain official membership in the 70s and 80s meant that you had to endure and survive a series of tests, ones that pushed you to the limits of personal endurance and perseverance. It was an absolute honor to be called a "Q" (the Greek symbol for Omega looks like the letter Q, so "Q" is the identification given to the frat's members) and your worthiness had to be tested through pledging. At the start of each academic year there would be a group of guys that each made a decision to be a part of the Omega Psi Phi fraternity. Those men made up the "line" of that particular year. Once the willing men were identified and the line was established, the pledging began. At the beginning of the academic year of 1976, I made it clear that I wanted to be a member of Omega Psi Phi. The line of '76 started out with thirty men who survived the first series of tests, but that number plummeted to three men as the challenges and trials of pledging weeded out the weak.

On the campus, there was a huge territorial rivalry between the boys from D.C. and the Baltimore boys, each tribe believing themselves to be superior. So when we three boys on the '76 line were all D.C. boys, and the line pledging us was made up of Baltimore boys, there were bound to be issues. Territorial rivalry ran deep. Even though we all wanted to be included in the same fraternity, it did not erase the tension over what turf was superior to the other.

One weekend during the pledging process of '76, the Baltimore boys sent us home for the weekend. When we returned to campus, ready to assume our pledging duties, we were shocked to find that the they'd dropped the line on us, meaning that they told everyone that we three pledgees had quit, dropped out, gave up, broke under the pressure. But that couldn't be less true. We three Bruhs (the name given to fraternity "brothers") endured eight weeks of pain and suffering—designed to symbolize the middle passage of slaves, where Black African men, women and children suffered and fought for their lives in the inner belly of slave transport ships—to be deemed worthy enough to stand for the Omega Psi Phi fraternity. We wanted to be black men who would stand to represent our brothers before us with loyalty and pride, and returning to campus to hear that those Baltimore dudes dropped the line on us was beyond infuriating.

The first thing I did when I got back to campus was find out which one of the Baltimore dudes had been responsible for lying and dropping the line on us. Initially, I kept his name a secret, but his identity became clear when I beat the hell out of him at a party the next weekend. Suffice it to say, there was a great deal of ass-whooping that went on after that controversy.

As you look back today, the line of 1976 is a 'ghost line,' meaning that the history books have no records of us guys who survived the pledging and were initiated into the fraternity, but now the world knows the truth. No way in hell did we drop the line: they dropped the line on us. This sort of behavior was nothing new for me. I knew what it was like to get all that you worked hard to achieve ripped from out under you. It hurt. It made me angry, but I kept it moving and eventually said, *Fuck it—I don't need to be a part of the fraternity. Whatever.*

Although I wasn't an official member of the frat, I spent most of my time around its organization and activities, as my closest friends were all Qs. After going through the drama of the 1976 pledging experience and being denied entry to the frat because of a lie, I was in no way looking for official inclusion from Omega Psi Phi. I had my friends—Stan, Sam, Jose, Ray, and Webb—and my girlfriend Stephanie, and I was fine with my life, working at the post office, continuing to run my miles, training in the gym. When I wasn't in class or working, I was at the library, reading, studying, and absorbing more information. I didn't need the frat. I was good without it.

In the spring of 1978, Stan came to me with a crazy question: "I'm pledging the frat. Want to pledge with me?"

"Fuck no," I said. "Are you crazy? Why in the hell would I put myself through that torture again? I had already proven myself once, so why should I have to do it again? I know I'm worthy. Fuck that." Stan said, "Come on man, do it with me." I didn't want to do it but, for Stan, I decided that I would.

So in the fall of 1978, I found myself pledging again, right alongside Stan. There was nothing they could do to break me. I had endured the 1976 ordeal, and this time would be no different. I can't give the details of the pledging activities because of our oath of confidentiality, but Charles

Darwin was right when he explained that only the strong survive. Put it this way: pledge and survive once, you are worthy to be a Q. Pledge and survive twice, you're a crazy muthafucka, more than worthy to be a Q. So there I was, an official member of the Omega Psi Phi Fraternity, crossing the line with five other worthy members: Stan Jackson, Mike Haywood, William Conley, Andre Davis, and Andrew Russell.

During my time at Maryland I learned a great deal about life. The things I didn't learn about at home as a child I learned through my relationship with my brothers in the frat as well as with the friends I'd met along the way. I learned about love, loyalty, friendship, and sacrifice. I learned that family is not necessarily friends, and friends are sometimes more family than the ones with which you share blood.

Until I met the brothers at Maryland, I didn't know what the motto, "Friendship is Essential to the Soul" really meant. To this day I have frat brothers who are family to me. We've stayed close because we endured the same pain and trials. Our bodies are branded with the Greek symbol Omega, to represent our allegiance to the frat and to each other. A piece of metal, shaped into the Omega symbol-Ω-was heated under fire until the metal burned bright orange-red. For us the metal was a coat hanger burning under the flames of a gas stove and pressed into the delicate flesh of our arms and legs. My skin singed and melted under the smoldering heat of the hot metal. The raw flesh would breed a scab that morphed into a scar, forever sealing the symbol of our loyalty to each other and to the legacy of Omega Psi Phi.

As brothers, we always had an agreement with one another whenever we would face any kind of trouble: if two people went in, two people came out or nobody came out—you never leave a brother behind, no matter what.

While it may seem most of our bonding happened through turmoil and confrontation, there was another side to the link. We learned poems and songs that were designed to uplift: "If" by Rudyard Kipling; "Invictus" by William Ernest Henley; "See It Through" and "Sermons We See" by Edgar Guest; and "The Bridge Builder" by Will Allen Dromgoole. When one person couldn't finish it, the other one would, serving as an example of the truth that this life was not meant to be lived alone.

Our frat chapter at U. of M. was called Crazy Chi Delta because we were a crazy group of men, living life on the edge: working hard and partying hard. Although we may have been as different as can be believed and as diverse as culturally possible, we were truly a band of brothers.

Fighting was just a way of survival, and although I had been accepted into a higher learning institution, my anger did not disappear. However, I was never the instigator. I tried to be unassuming, calm, and I always dressed nice, trying to look like I stepped out of a magazine shoot. The thing is: dudes heard of me and had to test me.

I would never be the first one to throw a punch since, because of my boxing training and expertise, my hands were technically registered with the state of Maryland as lethal weapons. If *I* delivered the first blow, it'd automatically be deemed an unfair fight. If they threw the first punch, my punches were merely self-defense. The fights were never really fights as much as they were simply ass-whoopings for the other man. Due to my frequent bouts on and off the campus, my reputation at the University of Maryland quickly became known to all.

There was always someone willing to test me. For example, take a dude named Iceberg Slim. Seven feet tall, and 250 pounds, Iceberg had a voice of pure bass that seemed to vibrate the walls when he spoke. He was a student at U. of M. and was often seen hanging out with the Baltimore dudes. He wasn't a part of the frat, but he was always around and, at that size, difficult to go unnoticed.

One extraordinarily cold winter day—we're talking ten degrees—my frat brothers Sam, Jose, Webb, and Luther, and I strolled into the campus union building. Once inside, Luther took off his warm winter gloves to put them in his pocket, then Iceberg Slim walked up, snatched them out of his hands and, with a sarcastic grin, said, "Thank you very much." After Iceberg ignored our demands to return Luther's gloves, I knew Iceberg was about to get his ass beat.

"You going to let that muthafucka take your shit? Just like that?" I asked Luther.

He said, "I ain't fighting him. Look how big that dude is. Fuck those gloves."

"Nah, I don't give a shit about that," I said. "I'm fighting him."

I didn't know how I would conquer this giant, but I knew I would. I jumped onto a stair, so I could be eye level with him. I gave his seven- foot frame a once-over, locating every major organ of his internal systems. With a kind of X-ray vision, I saw his heart, located in the fifth intercostal space.

Two punches there, and the heart would skip a beat, causing ventricular or atrial fibrillation. The xiphoid process would knock the wind out of him immediately. Scanning further down, I saw his liver, located on the right side of his abdominal cavity. Fierce contact there would release bile into his blood stream, causing him to piss blood. If I hit him with an uppercut punch under the bridge of his nose, bone spurs would shoot into his brain, causing paralysis, brain damage, or immediate death. If I hit him dead center between the eyes, I would cause an electric shock to pulsate through his head, blinding him and shattering the orbital bones and retinas of his eyes.

All this flashed before me in a matter of mere seconds, unfortunately for Iceberg, he didn't have a chance. I felt like David facing Goliath: when everyone else stood down, I stood up and said, "Send me."

Iceberg Slim knew very well who I was and what I was capable of doing to him. I knew he'd seen me beat the shit out of someone at a party just a couple months prior to our meeting on the union stairs. Since he was a foot taller than me, he figured I wouldn't be able to destroy him. But I could. And I would.

I gave him one last chance. "Give Luther the fucking gloves back."

He cocked his head to the side and said, "What, motherfucka?"

"You heard me."

And that was all it took for him to launch towards me, swinging his right hand as hard as he could straight at my face. Simple physics says that all you have to do is move centimeters out of the way of an object coming toward you to lessen its impact, or cause it to miss you completely. And when you combine the force of the punch with the mass of a 250-pound man, you know that a missed right jab will send him falling forward onto the steps. He landed right beside me–a perfect position for me to mess him up.

I yanked him up from the stairs, shoved him back against the wall, and hit him with a six-punch combination to the left side of his face, then immediately came through with a hard left hook to the right side of his body. He screamed in agony as he doubled over in pain. Campus security rushed around the corner, yelling to break up the fight. Still doubled over, Iceberg waved his arms in defeat and said, "Luther, take your fucking gloves, man." I shook my head with a slight grin across my face and my frat brothers laughed at the huge badass's humble, weak apology. The Goliath was defeated and the gloves were back in the hands of the rightful owner. Iceberg Slim didn't fuck with us again. He learned his lesson.

I practiced fighting because I wanted to be the baddest killer with precision of a master. I stayed up late at night, reading books about the human anatomy, books about ninjas, samurais, and ancient warriors. I learned the physics of fighting, and understood the power that comes with a full comprehension of how the laws of nature work for and against you in times of battle. I loved the thrill of the fight, the adrenalin surging through my veins, the sweat rushing to escape my tingling body. The sensation of hitting someone on the chin, the vibrations coming up my arm, shattering the person's cheekbone, was the ultimate thrill for me.

The anger was like a drug.

The year was 1979. I was twenty-two years old.

One night in the fall of '79, my frat brothers Sam and Jose were hanging out with me and Stephanie in her dorm room in Denton Hall on the south side of the Maryland campus. Stephanie and her friends were members of our sister sorority, so they often hung out with us Omega Psi Phi brothers.

I first met Stephanie at a party in the summer of 1978 and our relationship quickly exploded into a whirlwind romance. I had many girlfriends, and rarely lacked women, but there was just something different about Stephanie. My first real love was a drop-dead gorgeous, blow-your-mind, straight-off-the-runway, bombshell. She was 5'8" with a lean, athletic build, smooth caramel skin, and the brightest, most beautiful honey brown eyes. She was the more beautiful, Afro-American twin of Ingrid Bergman (Ilsa, from Casablanca, one of my favorite movies of all time).

After leaving Stephanie's dorm room that night, I walked down the eighth floor hallway and ran into my frat brother Rodney and his friend Snazz. Now Snazz was from Baltimore, and the rivalry and tension between the D.C. and Baltimore boys was still thick. Territorial rivalry doesn't die quickly, if ever. It's one of those things that runs deep within the blood. I had no quarrel with Snazz because I trusted Rodney—that is, up until Rodney introduced us and Snazz cocked a fist, reared back, hit me in my eye, and said, "Yeah, muthafucka. You box. Come on."

The world came to a screeching halt. Snazz had unknowingly unleashed the demon inside of me, the little boy who vowed that there would be no more hitting, no more slaps, no more beatings, whips, belts. No more betrayals. No more pain. My only thought was, I am going to kill this muthafucka.

I lunged forward, only to be grabbed by Rodney and my other frat brothers. They wouldn't let me get to Snazz, probably because they saw my bloodshot eyes and could feel my rage. I was using everything in me to escape from their grasp, all while yelling, "Come on, muthafucka! Come on!" But I couldn't break free.

In the meantime, some of the other residents in the hallway called the campus police. The cops showed up to the sight of a crazed man, yelling and screaming at the top of his lungs to be released from the grasp of three other dudes.

My fight to be released had exhausted my brothers and I suddenly tore free from their hands and down the hall after Snazz, yelling, "Get back here muthafucker," as the campus police chased after me. I swung open the stairway door—with every intention to chase Snazz down eight flights of stairs—but the cops had anticipated such a chase and positioned their last man just behind the stair entrance. As I flung the door open, I was hit in the shin with a baton, forcing me to my knees. Before I could get up, the other cops reached the door, grabbed me, tied my hands behind my back, and forced me to sit in the stairwell of the dormitory.

If it weren't for the cops, I'm confident that Snazz would have died that night.

This altercation caused such a stir around the school that the leaders of my own fraternity kicked me off campus, claiming that I was going to fuck up the charter for the fraternity. It's easy to call on the fighter when you are about to get your ass beat—I protected them and fought for them more times that I can count—but now, instead of standing up for me, they told me I was no longer welcome.

Reluctantly I left the frat house, saying to myself, "Fuck this shit." I acted like I didn't care, but it hurt. It cut deep. Being exiled from campus, I snuck into the dorm room with Stephanie and stayed with her for a while. However, I couldn't sleep at night, because all I could think about was getting back to Snazz. I stayed awake thinking about how I could destroy him, how I could make him suffer, make him feel the most excruciating pain and suffering that a human being could ever experience. There is no way that I would let him get away with what he did to me.

Three weeks later, I went to a party on the other side of campus, strictly because Stephanie told me that Snazz would be there. Stephanie lived with my turmoil and rage, seeing me awake night after night, twisting the horrid thoughts of murdering Snazz over and over in my mind. She knew the suffering that I was enduring, trying to control my desire for revenge. It was eating away at me, consuming my every thought. Stephanie knew that I wouldn't let this die until I was able to come face to face with Snazz and settle it once and for all.

Before I went on my Snazz hunt, she looked me in my eyes and said, "Be smart. Be smart about it." I nodded and left the dorm room immediately, heading straight to the party. I walked into the party house, where everyone was drunk, high, or both. Unch, my frat brother, met me at the door. Even though I'd been kicked off campus by the higher ups of the fraternity, my close frat brothers stood by me. Unch said, "They don't want me to tell you, but Snazz is right outside."

As soon as I saw Snazz in the backyard, I knew it was over for him. When he saw me, his eyes opened wide, revealing the terror deep inside of him. I could smell his fear. I slowly, calmly, walked over to him, looked him in the eye and said, "We ain't fighting right here because someone will break it up. Meet me on the golf course at 2:00 AM." The golf course would be neutral territory.

A couple hours later, I was at the 15th hole with my frat brother, Jose, and, right on time, Snazz ambled over with one of his frat brothers. To make sure it was a fair one-on-one fight, Jose followed Snazz into the woods and Snazz's boy followed me. It was like the gladiators walking to the coliseum of Rome. It was on: mano y mano.

I was ready to destroy Snazz, but he had to swing the first punch, and he did. This time his punch did not connect. The only way Snazz could ever manage to hit me was if he caught me off guard, like he did three weeks earlier. When he swung his fist toward me, I unleashed my fury on his ass. I was like Billy the Kid: the fastest gun in the West. People always asked Billy to draw, thinking they might be the one to finally bring him down. But always before the opponent could actually draw his gun Billy The Kid would have unloaded six rounds into him. It almost wasn't fair. Likewise, it only took a few minutes for me to finish Snazz. He fell to the ground, unable to get up. It was no longer a fight. I stood over him and wondered, *Should I kill him or not?* Then I remembered Stephanie's words to me before leaving her dorm, "Be smart."

Right then, from the corner of my eye, something caught my attention. I jerked my head up and, staring back at me, was that bright star. It's like that damn star was following me. It had to mean something. Breathing in and exhaling out, my anger and rage disappeared, replaced with a quiet peace.

I looked down at Snazz and he didn't even look human. Both of his eyes sockets were puffy and swollen shut, his front teeth were missing, and his broken jaw made his mouth hang open. Blood stained his clothes and his face, covering him in a crimson blanket. I had a choice to make: leave him for dead, or carry him back to safety. I decided I didn't want to leave my kill there for another animal to consume, so, without saying a word, I picked his up his weak, bloodied body, threw him over my shoulder, and hauled him over to his friend. Knowing the damage was severe, I said, "Take your boy to the hospital."

I later learned that Snazz needed extensive plastic surgery to repair the damage to his face. I never saw him again.

Although many of my college days were about fighting, drugs and women, the burning desire to find a greater purpose never disappeared. Amid all the violence, I often found myself staying up late at night, the dark hours holding too many horrid memories for me to sleep. During those long nights, I read and studied, taking in as much knowledge about the world as I could.

People didn't know this about me. They thought I was just the dumb ass fighter.

I took advantage of the library at U. of M.—the knowledge housed in that building was almost overwhelming. Walking into the library, you were drowned in book, papers, journals, periodicals, and movies on endless topics. At first, I studied kinesiology, biology, physics, and biomechanics of the human body to learn how to hurt people more accurately and efficiently. Then it led me to want to know more about botany, horticulture, art history, philosophy, and religion. The subject didn't matter: hungry for more information and knowledge, I read whatever I could get my hands on.

This was the ultimate duality. When I wasn't exacting hurt and revenge upon other people, the dudes that wanted to fight me around campus, I read texts like Newton's *Principia* and Aristotle's *Nicomachean Ethics*. I realized that I was standing with one foot on each side of the fence, sometimes flowing right, sometimes left. Without this duality, my life would be unfulfilled. I would never be able to appreciate the mountaintop without the valley, or the sunshine without the rain, or the food without the famine. How then could I appreciate life without having been on the brink of death? How could I know what it meant to be good without dealing in evil?

I felt most alive when I recognized these two equally potent forces, forces that possessed the power to dominate my life. I realized I had a choice as to who I was to become, but the conflicts wouldn't cease. I knew I would have to keep fighting, but perhaps instead of the physical fights, I'd have to fight the inner demons that tried to pull me down into hell on earth. I knew that in order to achieve what I desired, I'd still have to prove that I was worthy for a higher calling.

8

MOVING ON

The year was 1980. I was twenty-three years old.

The boiling, humid moisture in the air floated around me like a cloud of water, making it difficult to breathe on the hotter-than-hot day. As I stepped into the wharf at Haines Pointe, the stink and odor almost knocked me over. Looking out over the water, I remained motionless, contemplating everything, the sun beating against my skin.

I still didn't understand why I had to endure such pain and heartache, but I knew I was alive and it was up to me to make something of myself. I noticed the boats docked and the people clamoring about, laughing, smiling, and seeming to enjoy life in Maryland. I couldn't understand their perspective. All I knew was that my time here was done. I turned and walked out from the wharf with no regrets, only a passion for going somewhere and making something of myself.

I took the bus to the airport and bought a one-way plane ticket to Los Angeles, California. I had no plans to come back. I just wanted to get away. For good. Looking out of the window at thirty thousand feet, I realized I had to map out my strategy for surviving in my new, uncharted land. "Invictus," by William Earnest Henley, which I had learned during my pledge time at Maryland, rang over and over in my mind:

> *Out of the night that covers me,*
> *Black as the pit from pole to pole,*

I thank whatever gods may be
For my unconquerable soul.
In the fell clutch of circumstance
I have not winced nor cried aloud.
Under the bludgeonings of chance
My head is bloody, but unbowed.
Beyond this place of wrath and tears
Looms but the Horror of the shade,
And yet the menace of the years
Finds and shall find me unafraid.
It matters not how strait the gate,
How charged with punishments the scroll,
I am the master of my fate:
I am the captain of my soul.

I arrived in Los Angeles to seventy-degree weather, clear blue skies, and a warm inviting sun. I caught the first bus that approached the airport bus stop. The sign said: PASADENA. I didn't know anything about Pasadena, California, but I thought, *Shit. That's as good a city as any.* I boarded the bus, found a seat, took a deep breath, and thought, *Here we go. Now what?*

But I trusted that the demon inside would take care of me, that, no matter what, I would survive. Yes, the demon had caused me much suffering and pain, but it also had protected me. The rage scared me, but it was also my friend, the one who saved me from harm and from danger. His motto is, *Yea, though I walk through the valley of the shadow of death, I fear no evil, because I'm the meanest muthafucka in the valley.*

To eat, I needed money. To get money, I needed a job. Perusing the Pasadena classified ads, I noticed a local high school was looking for a security guard to work the day shift. I applied for the job but, before I could start, I had to take a test that all state-employed protection officers are required to pass, a test designed to discover the finest of the force, to weed out those who were unfit for the responsibilities. I breezed through it, passing the exam with the highest score in the history of the program, ultimately scoring a better salary than many of the other guards who had been on the force for a while.

Just like that, I was a well-paid security officer in Pasadena.

I moved out of the local motel and into my own two-bedroom

apartment. Not forgetting all of my diligent training over the years, I joined the local Gold's Gym and frequented it daily. The dudes that I met in Gold's were the truth—they believed in getting it in, working out hard, and lifting heavy. Many of the guys were convicts who had just been released from prison, and we got along well. They quickly realized my East Coast ways combined with my attraction to mortal combat was better to partner with than to resist. I became close with many of the dudes from the gym but, however close I became, I was still the new man to the group.

Watchdogs for the streets reported around Pasadena that there was a new muthafucka on the streets who needed to be tested. Just like the tension between people on the East Coast, the West Coast was no different with it cliques, gangs, groups, and clubs. I wanted nothing to do with the fighting and turmoil of Pasadena, but I wouldn't bow out on who I really was as a Warrior. By whatever means necessary, I would survive.

In the midst of all this, a man named Harold Jackson came to the school and said, "I need you to get me a job here."

I told him that I wasn't the person who hired people, that he needed to see someone else about that. But he wouldn't stop bothering me about the job, so finally I told him, "Cut to the chase, Harold. What do you want with me?"

Turns out, Harold Jackson was sent to watch me. Who sent him? I still don't know, but there he was. His duty was to make sure I was thorough, worthy to be feared in the streets of Pasadena. It didn't take long until dudes, once again, started testing me. Harold and I formed a bond as friends that carried me through to the next phase of my life.

9

INTERLUDE

Tonight I killed a man.

Tonight, I murdered a man in cold blood.

He's not the first and he won't be the last.

I can't stand to see women who are mistreated and children who are abused. The evil ones who abuse others should be scourged from this Earth.

I know the world and its perfect society says killing is wrong. But sometimes, it's right.

After all I've been through in my life, I have every reason to be angry and hate the world. My life hasn't been fair, hasn't been good, and hasn't been anything that I would wish upon another human being. Thinking about my journey often makes me think of killing.

And I do.

I need the release.

I've never been caught because I'm brilliant in my planning and strategic in my methods. I stay under the radar and people go missing. But I'm never even suspected. I'm a Master.

You want a recount of what happened tonight? First off, all my anger, hurt, rage, turmoil, and revenge turned into ecstasy when I carried out my deed. I achieved my greatest pleasure. I am alive today. Ah, the thrill of it! He deserved it. How dare he strike a child. What did the child do to deserve to be hit so hard as to fly to the ground and bust his head open? The man had no idea I was watching him. I tracked him. I followed him like a hawk. I saw him strike the boy on more than one occasion. His time couldn't come soon enough.

It's 9:00 PM. I know the man walks from his office to his car located around the block. He always parks in the same spot. I wait behind the trash dumpster and, as he approaches his car, I step out from the dark, holding an axe in my right hand. I hear the sounds of cars whizzing by on the nearby freeway. I smell the stench of the waste overflowing from the nearby trash bins. My grip tightens around the handle of my axe and I swallow hard as my thoughts flow to the inevitable gratification of his death.

My victim's eyes are frozen in fear. My heart is racing. Sweat is flowing from my brow as adrenaline oozes from my tear ducts and the pores of my caramel skin. I look directly into the man's soul through his pupils. The street lamp illuminates our world. His cheekbones are high. The brows on his face are thick, shading the lids of his soul-bearing windows. His face is weathered. The sun has stained his skin with patches of brown and yellow. His mouth is open. His bottom lip quivers as fear grips every morsel of his being. He is frozen in time, staring, standing still.

I take one step closer to him. I want him to fight back. I want him to run. I want him to try to escape my vengeance—that would only make it sweeter to me. But no, he doesn't. He is a coward, as I suspected. He is a high- powered security guard but he can't even protect himself. He abuses his wife and son, and I am here to take one living form of evil from the world.

Suddenly, he moves his right arm inside his jacket and, immediately, I lung forward like a lion attacking a gazelle. My axe moves through the air with enough velocity and force to destroy the concrete barricade fixed around the dumpster. In the second it takes for the axe to descend , I sense his animalistic fear of death. As my eyes fixate on his, I smell the hormones dripping from his body. Like an electric shock through my hands, the axe vibrates violent pulses as it slices directly through the man's skull.

He falls to the ground.

He is dead.

I stand tall, chin high and shoulders pressed back, and sigh with relief.

The world is now a better place. The man will no longer abuse his wife or his son.

His evil has been eliminated .

I walk away from the scene with no feelings of remorse, only pure satisfaction at my good deed of the day. Sure, maybe some people loved the man. Perhaps his son was looking forward to his return tonight. Maybe his wife had made him a lovely dinner. But all that bullshit of the niceness of the world only clouds people's judgments of themselves and others. We need to see the world for what it is. I should be awarded a crown tonight. Because I am the King.

No cops. No chase. No record of my ever being in the man's presence. I'll see it on the 11 o'clock news tonight. The media will hype it up as if this man were Gandhi or someone who had brought something good into the world. See—that's what I am trying to say. People need to see the world for what it is. My contribution is to kill those bastards. If nothing else, it makes me feel better about myself. And, after all, who else matters in this world but me? I am the master and all will bow down to me!

But I must confess this is not a confession.

This is not the truth.

The story is believable. It is who I feel I should be. It is who I fight to keep from becoming.

10

REVISIT THE PAST

I was settling in well to Pasadena.

I had a job, a house, money, and a vast array of friends: gangsters and robbers, preachers and teachers. I also kept up with my friends and my frat brothers back in Maryland—Jose, Sam, Stan, Luther, Cozy, and Derrick among them— but one of my best friends from Maryland was my boxing pal Ray, a.k.a., Sugar Ray Leonard.

Sugar Ray was born Ray Charles Leonard on May 17, 1956, in Rocky Mount, North Carolina. He was the fifth of seven children born to Ciero and Getha Leonard. His family moved to Washington D.C. when he was three years old, eventually settling in Palmer Park, Maryland. He was my neighbor from the time we both starting walking, but we didn't meet until Ray started his boxing training at the Palmer Park Rec Center in 1969, following in the footsteps of his brother Roger. When Ray came on the scene, we connected immediately. We trained together, running our daily roadwork stride to stride, and often asked Mr. Jacobs to put us together in the sparring routine. We were tight.

Although my boxing career had been cut short, I remained close with Ray and continued training alongside him. He went on to win the National Golden Gloves in 1973 and 1974, and the amateur boxing world became enamored with his sheer athleticism. In 1976, when Ray made the U.S. Olympic team as light welterweight representative, I knew I'd be joining him on the trip as his official training partner. It was an honor to be there because the 1976 U.S. Olympic team—Ray Leonard, Leon and Michael Spinks, Howard Davis, Jr., Leo Randolph, Charles Mooney, and John Tate—has been justifiably hailed as the greatest in the history of the Olympics.

The days leading up to the bouts were filled with anticipation and chaos, but we were more than ready for the competition. Ray won his first four fights by 5-0 decisions before facing Kazimier Szczerba in the semifinals, another 5- 0 decision. In his final bout, Ray met Cuban superstar and knockout fighter Andres Aldama. With several great left hooks in the first round, and, later, a left to the chin, Ray dropped Aldama to the mat. Surviving the eight count, Aldama rose slowly to his feet. With only a few seconds left in the fight, Ray knocked him to the mat again, securing his last and final win for the gold.

After Ray's victory, it was pure pandemonium. With the crowd still cheering, Ray and I ran from the Olympic stadium, screaming and hollering and waving our hands in the air, running a lap of victory around the outside of the stadium, around the parking lots filled with mobile camping trailers serving as houses for the family and friends of Olympic athletes. We barged into one of the mobile trailers chanting, "Champ, Champ, Champ!" The startled people soon realized it was Ray Leonard and shouted, "We just saw you on TV! You are the champ!" Nobody was mad. It was just a couple of young, crazy kids from Palmer Park taking the world by storm.

After I moved west, Ray and I still stayed close. Throughout the years, we'd spent countless months training, running thousands of miles in the oxygen- depraved conditions of high altitude environments, sparring for hours on end, sharpening our minds, and conditioning our bodies to ultimate perfection. I was the one by his side when nobody else would lace up their boots for 5:00 AM roadwork. I was the ultimate believer in Sugar Ray Leonard. Little wonder then that geographical distance wouldn't break our bond.

Around March of 1986, during one of our many phone calls, Ray told me that he'd just watched the talented champion Marvin Hagler knock out John "The Beast" Mugabi, and he knew he could beat Hagler, no question about it. Soon afterwards, Ray announced to the world that he would return to the ring to fight Hagler on April 6, 1987 at Caesars Palace in Las Vegas. The next month, when Ray told me, "Darrell, I need you again," I knew the time was right for us Warriors to reunite. After all, I was the guy that Ray always trusted when he needed someone to help get him to the world-class level necessary to win belts. Although he had become quite famous and revered, I still treated Ray like he was the same dude I knew in Palmer Park. There was a level of trust between us, that all of his new sparring and training partners just couldn't emulate. It was a brother-like bond, one that Ray called upon when he needed that extra edge, that something to push him to be the absolute best. There was no doubt that I had to return to the East Coast and train with Ray for this upcoming, career-defining bout with Hagler. We had a year to prepare for what the promoters were calling "The Super Fight," so I took a leave of absence from my job and flew back east, back to the pain of my childhood, back to a place I never wanted to see again. I did it for Ray.

The official training camp in Hilton Head, South Carolina, wouldn't kick off until closer to the fight date, but we weren't taking any chances. We were going to be more prepared than we had ever been before, so I set up my own personal training camp in Maryland inside the living room of my Omega brother Sam Northington's house. That training camp was as intense as any professional training camp that ever existed before or after for either Ray or myself.

I limited my exposure to outside influences, like TV or movies. I controlled my diet, eating mostly steamed or raw vegetables, lean meat, and grilled chicken. I woke up every morning at 5:00 AM to meet Ray for roadwork. It was always five miles and, regardless of the weather, we ran in combat boots. The run was hard enough, but the combat boots made the training even more difficult. But our training was never meant to be easy, in any way. It was meant to craft and mold us into lean, mean, fighting machines, able to meet the meanest, maddest, most conditioned fighter in the ring—and come out on the other end victorious. Those heavy combat boots were a constant reminder that winning the fight is never simple and it takes doing what other people won't do in order to come out on top. I knew that I had to be better than the person with whom I was training. I had to be the one pulling him to greatness, so my goal was perfection. I wouldn't stand for anything less.

This training time was about focus, and no distractions would be tolerated. Nobody was allowed to set foot into the camp, not even Sam's girlfriend (who lived in the house). Sam protected me like a lion, demonstrating both his belief in who I was and his bond with me as a brother. He knew how important this was to me, so he gladly gave up his time and resources to help me achieve my goal. He kept his house quiet, provided me with a bed, a shower, and access to his washing machine and dryer. He made sure that I had everything that I needed to properly prepare for our inevitable victory.

Ray and I trained in Maryland until the twelve weeks leading up to the fight, when we moved in Hilton Head, where we ran our five miles in combat boots each day on the beach. We engaged in gut wrenching sparring sessions, which led to black eyes from right jabs, cuts from left crosses, and shits and pukes from countless body shots.

Shortly before a major prizefight, the sanctioning boxing commission can require the principle fighters to report to the state where the fight will take place in order to complete final drug testing. So, the last two weeks before the fight, I walked around Las Vegas wondering, *Why are there so many people here? Who are they? Don't they have to work?* It felt strange, but in the desert, everything felt strange. Molecules in the atmosphere had changed. Everybody and their brother was coming to Vegas. I know why we were there. We had to be there—we were present day Gladiators, fighting our way out of the ghetto. But I couldn't grasp why so damn many other people were compelled to be there. Doctors, lawyers, politicians, farm workers, clergymen, all of the top entertainers and movie stars, pimps, pushers, drug dealers, cops and robbers: they were all in Vegas. They had dropped their everyday family lives and jobs so they could migrate to one common place with one common goal to see *The Fight*. I guess everybody loved Ray as much as I did.

Two days before the fight, Ray beat the hell out of three of his sparring partners, and I knew he was ready. His hands were fast, he was hitting hard, floating around the ring like he was dancing on air. Hagler was in trouble.

And then it was April 6.

I trained for this fight like it was mine, like it would be me in that ring destroying Marvin Hagler, but I knew that when that bell rang, Ray was alone, and alone was a place I know all too well. But being a part of this team made me feel a part of something much bigger. Through Ray, I could pretend that family and friends were rooting for me, not breaking my trophies, not destroying my spirit. That's one of the reasons why I pushed him so hard, because I still wanted to be associated with someone who the world actually cared about.

A slew of parked luxury cars—Rolls Royces, Bentleys, Maseratis, Lamborghinis, Mercedes Benzs—blocked the entrance to Caesars Palace, in front of a façade reminiscent of the ancient pillars of the coliseum of Rome. The marquee read:

The Super Fight

MARVIN HAGLER (62-2-2, 52 KO, WBC Titleholder)
vs.
SUGAR RAY LEONARD (33-1, 24 KO)

There were 15,000 people in attendance, and over 400 million people in over fifty countries watching on television. The whole world had been anticipating this moment for over four years—and it was time.

Everyone who loved and supported Ray was there: his brothers, Roger and Kenny; his sister Bunny; his mom and pop; everybody. And it was like a satellite family for me. I knew Ray was going to beat Hagler because everyone that loved him was there.

There was no way he wouldn't win that night.

With all the people, the music, the lights, the camera flashes, my senses were on fire as the adrenaline coursed through my body. Mobs of security surrounded us as we made our way down the narrow hallway leading to the outdoor arena. Ringside, the team who had been training for months was now replaced by the suits and the cigars there to bask in the fight's pomp and circumstance.

Arriving ringside, Ray slipped through the ropes and jumped into the ring. The ring's blue mat was marked with the red Budweiser logo, a Caesar's Palace logo right below it. Wearing his newly designed, pristine white robe with the words "Sugar Ray" stitched in red on the back, Ray moved around the ring, light on his feet, bobbing and weaving, throwing punches into the air, mentally preparing to dominate the 24' x 24' battlefield.

And I was right there, picturing myself in the ring, getting ready to destroy Hagler.

Deep down, all I really ever wanted was to be the Champ. I wanted the recognition and the praise for being the best in the world, and now even more than ever. I regretted the night I was disqualified and shunned from the sport that I learned to love. I thought about how it would have all been different, how my life would have turned out if I'd been able to control myself on that night. But I knew I couldn't go back and change what had been done, so I took a deep breath, clenched my fist, caught Ray's eyes, and nodded for him to destroy that muthafucker.

We'd learned that Hagler was highly insulted that Ray challenged him to a fight after taking off four years, so insulted that he had murder on his mind. Hagler thought of Ray as a pretty boy, but he didn't know that Ray has had one of the most excruciating fighting camps of his life and was coming into the ring ready to fuck him up. We were there to whip his ass using the sweet science of boxing.

Flanked by his camp and all the dignitaries, Marvin Hagler joined Ray in the ring, after which World Boxing Council announcer Chuck Hull walked to the center of the ring, grabbed hold of a microphone, and roared: "This is the main event of the night. Twelve rounds of boxing for the WBC middleweight championship of the world. Introducing, in the blue corner, fighting out of Potomac, Maryland. Weighing in at 158 pounds with a professional record of 33 wins, 1 defeat with 24 KOs. He is the challenger and former undisputed welterweight champion of the world: Sugar Ray Leonard!"

The stadium vibrated under my feet as the 15,000-strong audience erupted with screaming and cheering. I turned around to look at the crowd as their deafening roar sent chills up my back. This was the moment that I had been preparing for and dreaming about for the last year.

After the stragglers were cleared from the mat, referee Richard Steele met Ray and Hagler in the center of the ring: "All right, listen," he said. "I gave both of you your instructions in your dressing rooms. I want to caution you again: obey my commands at all times. Shake hands—and good luck." And off they went.

Our team's plan was this: go into the ring in control and disarm Hagler physically and emotionally and make him beat himself. It's all about precision and hitting to the solar plexus and fifth intercostal space of the body to make bald-ass Hagler's heart skip a beat. Fight with disdain—compassion in the ring is the enemy. Take no prisoners. If you are throwing your hands at me, you get punches coming back. Anytime you throw a punch at me, you have to bring ass to get ass. You are compromising your defense. Hagler was the modern day Jake Lamotta, and he's going to get his ass beat like he stole something. Ain't nobody going into the ring scared of him.

Hagler's plan was to fight like an orthodox fighter instead of like the southpaw he was. Didn't work. He lost the first four rounds. But he didn't give up. Round after grueling round, the fighters used every ounce of strength and tenacity to pound each other. I was in Ray's corner, moving, analyzing, and following Ray's every punch, move, and tilt. Ray was like a panther playing with his prey. He got tired, naturally—Hagler was a beast, after all—but all those miles, all that physical conditioning, and all our training had prepared him. With a smile on his face, he moved around the ring as Hagler chased after him, the crowd chanting, "*Sugar Ray. Sugar Ray.*"

I could almost hear what was going through his head: if I can get you to follow me around the ring, you are a sucker. Come get this ass whooping.

With less than a minute left to go in the twelfth round, Ray waved his right arm in the air, shuffled his feet back and forth quickly, paying homage to Ali, Robinson, and the great ring generals from the past who'd showed him the way. He thanked God nobody got hurt, took a deep breath, and wiped a tear from his eye, because he already knew he had won the fight. The final bell rang and both men approached their respective corners, raising their gloves to the sky, claiming their victory.

Ray's whole team readied themselves to climb into the ring and celebrate the victory—but not me. I took a quiet moment for myself, closed my eyes, and let out a deep breath of gratitude and relief, because I knew the battle had been won. I then turned around to the stands to acknowledge the sparring partners, the equipment guys and all the others who were part of Ray's victory. Although they didn't have ringside seats, they were just as much part of the success as anyone else in our camp. They were our family, as important to me as anything or anybody.

If the universe did not give me a functional family, I decided I would have to create my own.

Over the years, I've learned a very important loyalty lesson: friends aren't necessarily family and family aren't necessarily friends. Relationships are about loyalty, integrity, and character. I wanted the guys who put in the hard work and long hours to trust me, always. We'd been through three months of pain together. I needed my shadow to match my shape, meaning that my image to the rest of the world must be the same when nobody was watching. I lived with integrity: I was the same person at all times to all people. I wasn't going to be friends with the rest of the team during practice and forget about them after the fight. It was important that they felt as much a part of the victory as anyone else.

After what seemed like an eternity, Chuck Hall finally took the mic to announce the results: "Ladies and Gentlemen, here is the decision of the judges. We have a split decision. Judge Lou Filippo scores the bout 115, Marvin Hagler; 113 Ray Leonard. Judge Joe Guerra scores the bout 118, Leonard; 110 Hagler. And Judge Dave Moretti scores 115, 113, the winner by split decision—and the new middleweight champion of the world—Sugar Ray Leonard!"

The people in that stadium and the millions watching around the world got the fight they wanted—and then some. Our passion for excellence had paid off. Here we were, a year after deciding to get back into the ring—a year of sacrifice, hard work, dedication, grueling training sessions, and miles and miles of roadwork—taking home that belt.

Ray's friends and family all gathered outside the locker room after the fight to congratulate the Champ. I saw Ray's mother looking through the crowd. When her eyes found me, she rushed toward me, wrapped her arms tightly around me, and said, "Thank you. You know you're my baby too." Those words, coupled with the pain of never hearing 'I love you' from my own mom, refueled my obsession to make it.

Ray and I met in the locker room, where we gave each other a hard fist pound and yelled, "We did it!"

Ray then said, "Yeah, man. I couldn't have done it without you."

Through a huge smile, I nodded. "You know I got you, man."

After this Super Fight, Marvin Hagler never fought again. He left the United States and moved to Italy, pissed off because he thought the fight was unfairly judged. Hagler lost both the physical and the psychological battle. The loss practically destroyed him. He quit. But not me, because, as the great author Napoleon Hill wrote, "Victory is always possible for the person who refuses to stop fighting."

11

HIDING

Training Ray was a double-edged sword.

Yes, walking away victorious was exhilarating, but being seeped in boxing brought the dark emotions of my childhood back to the surface. There were times during that year-long training camp that I lost touch with reality, allowing the dark recesses of my soul to bubble up the furious power and rage that boiled inside. This aggression to kill, the murderous feeling of chaos, is the very thing that made me a beast. I acknowledged the darkness inside me and allowed it to control me for times of war, when compassion is always a weakness. It comforted me at night knowing that I feared no evil because the mean muthafucka inside me was wide-awake.

When the scales are titled, when the demon is ruling, a life outside of fighting ceases to exists. The day after the fight, the war was no longer an external battle but an internal struggle between that ravenous beast looking for a kill and the higher man that sought to rise above his pain and suffering. I felt the same urgency to get the hell away from my past as I did when I left Maryland in the first place.

Returning to California, I knew I had get back on my own journey. I felt as if I had been tricked into returning to something that held such a strong bondage over me and my life. Sure, I had willingly returned east to train Ray, but it was like a sweltering pot of pain had just been stirred around, bubbling the rage to the surface again.

The weather changed. Songs came on the radio. Events began to unfurl all over the world. Chaos. Big things. Small things. And I was just starting to notice all the stuff of life. A woman's heel breaking off of her shoe. A man spills his coffee. A truck tire blows. A siren sounds from out of nowhere. A kid drops his icy pop and whines.

I was too awake.

Around then, I read somewhere, "You must heed the omens." I figured that this must be some sign for me, I just wasn't sure exactly what it all meant. I felt out of balance, out of sync with who I was and what I was supposed to be doing with my life.

To regain some sense of control, I went back to the thing that saved me in the first place: running. I laced up my shoes, got in my car, and drove to the Rose Bowl Stadium in Pasadena, located just a few miles from my apartment. I parked, got out, and just took off. I ran to escape, to clear my head. As I was reliving the feeling of the past, the victory of Ray's fight, the hours, days, and months of preparation and dedication, I had an epiphany: fuck boxing. Fuck hitting people. Fuck people hitting me. I wanted to get as far away from boxing as possible. I felt like boxing was the catalyst for the resurfacing of the memories that I had worked so hard to suppress. If I walked away, maybe I could finally move on with my life.

I'd started boxing at such a young age and, from that point on, my life had been all about fighting, hurt, and pain. But after Leonard/Hagler, I got to the a point where I didn't even want to watch the sport on television. I had been through all the fighting and the violence and beating the hell out of everyone, and it always led back to the little demon inside whose walls of steel lined the inner crevices of my heart. Boxing at that point had become non productive, so I rebelled against my skill to fight and hid away in a regular job.

In an effort to expand my knowledge of life, to learn the ways of the world, and to figure out some of the sciences and complexities of human nature, I landed in an Emergency Medical Technician class at UCLA. I had already spent long hours studying the structure and workings of the human body, so this material was second nature to me. Nonetheless, there was plenty to learn.

The human body is the perfect illustration of separate components working together to make a whole. There are many analogies for the human body, but the one that grabbed me was the one articulated in Atul Gawande's book The Checklist Manifesto: most buildings and master architects base their projects on the human body. They all have plumbing, which is the vascular system. They all have ventilation, which is the respiratory system. They all have electrical systems, which is the nervous system of the human body. It's amazing how our everyday external experiences are influenced by the intricate and perfectly designed human body. Being an EMT would fit me perfectly.

I landed a job as an on-site EMT at the Disney Imagineering Manufacturing Plant in Tujunga, California, where they built the amusement park rides. I'd never been to an amusement park before—hell, I didn't even remember ever having any real toys as a child. Seeing the construction of the massive toys that people would drive hundreds of miles to pay hundreds of dollars to enjoy showed me a small part of what I had missed. I vowed that I would have the things that I wanted in life despite not having a wealthy, loving upbringing. Who knows? Maybe I would run Disney one day and be able to give back to the kids in the ghetto, to offer them something.

While working as an EMT I continued my studies to become a certified personal trainer through the American Council of Exercise. All of the training and coaching that I had done in my lifetime was spent working with elite athletes and world class fighters, and I didn't have experience working with people who didn't share the commonality of lifelong, intense, all-or-nothing commitment for optimal physical and mental fitness, so this job pushed me out of my comfort zone, forcing me to see other people's perspectives on, not only training, but life as well.

I still had no desire to be associated with boxing and fighting. In the gym, people would stop by and ask, "Didn't I see you on TV with Sugar Ray Leonard?" but I tried to hide from my past. I didn't want anyone to recognize me, to stimulate the rage. I wanted a normal life, outside of all that. At least, that's what I thought.

12

MY PEACE

The year was 1998.

Up to this point everything in my life had been about surviving and fighting, fighting and surviving. Desperate to control my passion for revenge, I found escape in little things like watching movies or running laps at the track, but I never really knew true peace. I didn't understand the peace that covers you like a warm blanket on a cold winter's night, or the peace that soothes the turmoil of blood that boils in anger, or the peace that supersedes the obstacles that life has handed out.

However, when it finally came to me, the windows of Heaven opened, and I realized there was the chance I'd know the one true peace with the power to blanket, soothe, calm, and restore my weary soul. My peace, my love, my rest from the fight, came in the form of a beautiful angel. Her name was Franca Campopiano.

Of all the things missing in my life, the absence of love carved the deepest wound. The times I wanted to cry out in pain, the days when I felt the weight of the world to be too heavy, the days that turned into years of inner turmoil and prison, and the nights when my heart would swell with the tears that I failed to cry—love could have covered them all. By whatever grace that I had been given, this girl would be the one to show me what it meant to love and, in turn, give me the freedom to learn to be loved in return.

When I met Franca, I wasn't looking for someone to complete me, or a relationship that would provide the sort of love I'd been denied. For that matter: I had no clue that I was missing anything at all. On a certain level I thought everything in my life was just fine. I had made it this far, so surely I wasn't missing any crucial element. However, I would soon learn that sometimes the thing that you need the most is the thing that you never knew you needed.

I first saw Franca in the gym. She was a perfect picture of a Warrior princess. She outran everyone on the treadmill in both speed and distance. She lifted the heavy iron in the weight room with all the dudes. She wasn't afraid of the challenge. She welcomed it. Her body was perfect. She was about 5'5" with an athletic build, 115 pounds of lean muscle mass, and only 8% body fat. Her performance on the treadmill told me that she was much more than a beautiful figure. She not only had the physical physique, but her condition on the inside matched that on the outside. She was training to become Ms. Fitness, winner of a national competition where women from all over the world compete and are judged in three rounds of competition: displaying competence and confidence, showing mastery of muscle conditioning and shaping of the physique and overall fit body, and displaying strength, flexibility, and endurance in an original fitness routine. A schoolteacher from Pasadena, she was as smart as she was beautiful— she'd already completed a master's degree and was working on her PhD in education. She'd accomplished so much in her life. Her zest and zeal were inspirational.

One day, when we happened to be walking into Gold's Gym together, I held the door open for her and asked, "You looking for me?"

The question hung in the air like a floating bubble as I watched a slight smirk roll across her lips. She'd seen me as many times as I'd seen her, and although this was the first verbal interaction, our eyes had surely met long before this day. We had one of those instant connections where the world slowed and the objects between us vanished as the magnetic draw of a cosmic connection pierced through our eyes into the windows of our souls.

Her hesitation to respond made me anxious, like this was a game, albeit a game I would gladly partake in. After a few seconds she said "No," but I was pleased because my little question was enough to get her to at least acknowledge me. Soon we were going out on casual lunches and, after a few conversations over egg whites with spinach and mushrooms, I knew I had to keep her in my life. Nothing was "official" about our relationship. I just loved spending time with her. We often met at the gym, running alongside one another in the mornings and lifting weights together in the afternoons. She became my friend, the one I could always count on to show up when nobody else was there. She had a light about her. She was that star in the midnight sky that helped me find my way.

One afternoon after a heavy lifting session in the gym, she took the initiative and invited me on a date. We had been out together many times before, but I knew this date was going to be different. The next Saturday, she picked me up and told me that our plans were a surprise. I reluctantly agreed, even though I hate surprises. I like to know what's going on at all times. But her glow was contagious, and I could tell this was something that was special to her, so I rolled with it.

She drove me to the park, pulled into the parking lot, and turned off the car. I looked at her kind of crazy, thinking that this couldn't be my surprise. She smiled and said, "We're here. Get out."

Confused, I said, "This is the surprise?"

Laughing, she nodded and said, "Yep!"

I looked around the parking lot at the other cars, noticing the kids playing on the swing sets and monkey bars off in the distance. I still didn't understand why we were there.

We walked around to the back of the car and she opened the trunk, then pulled out a basket and a blanket. I thought, *What the hell are we going to do with that?* She must have sensed how uncomfortable I felt in that moment because she grabbed my hand and said, "Come on, we are going to have a picnic."

I said, "No. Let's go get something to eat at the restaurant, not here." She smiled, then started walking toward the green grass that covered the grounds of the park. I followed after her, holding her hand, decided to go along with it.

Now I had heard of people having picnics in the park, but I never knew anyone who'd actually done it. That was on television. When we got to a spot she was comfortable with, she laid out the blanket and starting taking the food from the basket. I thought, *What kind of bullshit is this?*

She patted the blue quilted fabric with the palms of her hands, inviting me to sit down on the blanket beside her. How could I not? She looked so beautiful hunkered down there as the soft wind blew her hair back from her face. I slowly lowered to my knees and felt the soft grass underneath the blanket. The smell of the woodsy red wine and fine cheese filled my senses.

Without saying a word, she gave me a handcrafted card covered with cut out pictures. I didn't know how to react. Nobody had ever made me anything before. Who was this chick? As I held the card, I looked at her warm brown eyes, smooth Italian skin, and long auburn hair, allowing it to soak in and take my breath away for a split second. All I could think was that she took the time to make this card, plan this date, and here we are, in the middle of a park, where anybody could drive up and shoot me. I was exposed (and obviously still hanging on to that ghetto mentality of, 'you'd better watch your back'). Suddenly, I accepted the richness of the moment and, thanks to this beautiful woman, began to feel safe.

That was only the beginning.

Our relationship quickly escalated as she became not only my friend inside the gym, but my best friend outside of it. She challenged me to think about life from a different perspective. She told me about her passion for educating underprivileged kids, and what it meant to give back to the world. She picked my brain about topics ranging from religion to politics, family values and athletics. She brought a peace to my life that I had never experienced before. She taught me what it meant to love, what it meant to be loyal, what it meant to sacrificially give yourself and your time to make a positive impact in one person's life and thus make the world a better place.

We moved in together, making our relationship "official," but soon her sense of perspective and her peace were tested, seeing how she had no idea who she had just tied herself to. Meanwhile, I had no idea that she would become my rock, but that's exactly what she became—and still is to this day.

While I loved her strong Italian name, I gave her the nickname "Piano," short for her last name (Campopiano), and ever since that date in the park, she's been my absolute best friend. To me, she's the ultimate Woman, the one who was sent to give me the light, the hope, and the love that I needed to keep moving on, to keep pressing to achieve what I desired, which was to gain freedom from the bondage of my childhood and to own the identity of someone who could overcome such circumstances and help other people in the world do the same.

13

DON'T GET READY, STAY READY

It soon became apparent that working at Disney wasn't what was truly in my heart.

Though helping people was satisfying, it was nothing more than a nine-to-five grind, a dead-end job. I was making minimal money, living paycheck to paycheck, and on top of that, the medical bills were piling up from a recent motorcycle accident. Although I made great strides in achieving a certain level of success, I still felt lost.

On the plus side, Disney brought me closer to an industry that I've been fascinated with since childhood: show business. I'd always had a great love for movies, and, as a child, when I wasn't watching *Leave It to Beaver*, I was submerging myself in the fantasy of film. I found comfort in movies because I could suspend my reality for a couple of hours and pretend to be someone else, someone living in a better world.

Stuck in the Disney grind, the world became dark again. I'd lost sight of the guiding star in the midnight sky. Where did it go? It seemed I had gained footing, but had I actually *regressed* in my ultimate journey? What had happened to my dreams of success? I would try to find quiet moments to be still and listen for the voice, but I heard nothing—and silence in a dark world is always scary. I looked in the mirror and asked myself, *Was the Monster right after all? Would I really never amount to anything?*

I was hiding, but at least at this point I knew it. I was dodging my bigger purpose, but I didn't want to face it. For all the wrong reasons that anybody stops doing the thing they love, I had stopped too. It was the thing that made me feel most alive, yet I gave it up. Why? I realized my world was dark because I was blocking the light with my own resistance. No matter how hard you try, you can't hide from your calling. It seeks you and, despite every effort you give to ignoring it, it's stays there.

But no matter how hard I tried to hide from boxing, it always found me. Even after I moved to the other side of the country, and even though I took a completely different direction, it always showed up. Despite being determined to make it in this world without having to revisit my pain and suffering, fate had another plan.

One day, as I was minding my own business, working as a security guard at a D.A.R.E. (Drug Abuse Resistance Education) fundraiser, someone from Shanghai'd Films approached me. He asked if I would come to a meeting about a movie, written and to be directed by Ron Shelton of *Bull Durham* fame.

I thought, *Hey—they want me to be a movie star. Cool.* I agreed. Two days later, I received a call with a request to meet the producers and principal actors of a film called *Play It to the Bone.*

I walked into the room, and there sat Shelton, Antonio Banderas, and Woody Harrelson. They greeted me warmly and invited me to sit at the round glass table in the middle of Ron's office. I checked out the memorabilia from *Bull Durham* and *Tin Cup* hanging on the walls, the twenty-five-year-old bottle of scotch on the table, and, to Ron's left, a huge stack of movie scripts. Turns out, they were about boxing. Apparently they had heard I had worked with Sugar Ray Leonard and now wanted me to train these guys for a film about fighting.

I thought to myself, *Now here comes Hollywood wanting me to make movies about boxing. What is this?* If I go to my car and turn on my radio, the song is going to be some country and western song about my baby done left me and took my boxing shoes. If I pick up a newspaper, they are going to be talking about some boxer who lost his car keys. Boxing, boxing, boxing.

But Shelton was a former professional athlete, and right off the bat we got along well. That's why I accepted the job. Despite my efforts to escape, I couldn't say no. So just like that, I became the boxing trainer for *Play It to the Bone.*

The movie was a sports drama about two boxers who happened to be best friends. It chronicles their journey to Las Vegas, where they would have to fight each other for the middleweight champion title. I loved the idea of the movie and the layers that the story revealed about the truths of universal human experience. The idea of having to meet your best friend in the ring meant having to relinquish the trust, love, and brotherhood that bonded you together as friends in the first place. I was excited to get involved in the movie industry and serve a part in telling this story, which featured not only Banderas and Harrelson, but wonderful people like Lolita Davidovich, Tom Sizemore, Lucy Liu, and Robert Wagner.

Ever since I had started working, I'd always fully committed to any job I took—and this project was no different. I understood that I had to look past my own personal struggles and difficulties of the duty at hand and focus on the greater good of the film. I enjoyed the job because it was something different from the daily grind, but I still hadn't quite figured out how to control the pain I associated with fighting and boxing. Even though I successfully carried out my duties as trainer, I was still committed to get away from fighting for good. I thought there had to be another path for me.

However, my calling persisted.

Soon after I settled back into my normal working routine as a security guard at Disney, I got word that Columbia Pictures was seeking a boxing trainer for an upcoming movie about Muhammad Ali's life starring Will Smith.

Ali was my hero. He represented so much for the world of boxing, for the world of Americans, and equality and freedom for all people. I remember growing up and watching Ali's fights on TV, longing for that kind of attention and praise. He offered a hope, an sense of optimism, a strength that indicated that you have choices about who you are and what you want to be in life. He was my inspiration in the ring, and meeting him, even if only briefly, was an encounter that I treasured deeply.

Even with the positive feelings that were associated with Ali, I just didn't want to go there again. The thought of boxing and fighting made me think of killing, and brought my mind back to the worst moments of my childhood, making me feel cornered and trapped.

I'd been conditioned to perceive everything as a threat. To this day, if someone as much as touches my back, my immediate reaction is to turn and punch them square in the face. There's no forethought to the decision. It's simply a survival mechanism for me. With all these feelings of hurt, pain, rage, turmoil, confusion, and anger, I had to take a long, hard look at myself and consider what I really wanted. I asked myself, *Did I really want to reach in and stir up the turmoil that I worked so hard to suppress?*

I was conflicted. On one shoulder, I heard, "No. Don't. It's not worth the pain." And on the other shoulder, a voice said, "You must. Life is bigger than your past." There was a battle for my soul. My world was dark and I felt like I was going nowhere, lost in a world without light. However, the more I thought about the possibility of doing this movie, I began to notice all the little things around me, things I had overlooked and ignored for so many years. I noticed the rose bush right outside my apartment, and the kids in the park playing. *Was that new?* I'd never even seen it before and I drove this way every day. Talking to people I worked with at Disney, I began noticing their eye colors: the most beautiful hues of brown, green, blue, and sometimes a mixture of all colors.

The world began to light up, and, as much as I wanted to deny it, I knew that this boxing job was exactly what I needed. Plus, it would offer me the opportunity to give back to Ali and his legacy.

The studio brought in the best fighters and boxing coaches in the world to audition for this coveted coaching job. This wasn't simply a boxing movie; this was *the* boxing move, the one featuring the greatest boxer of all time. This would be a multimillion-dollar project starring the biggest actor in Hollywood.

The producer's plan was to hire three different people to work with Will Smith: one for strength and conditioning, one for health and nutrition, and one for boxing training. Thanks to my previous experiences as a professional fighter and with my training camps working with Sugar Ray Leonard the studio quickly realized that I could be all three people in one.

The studio set up an interview for me with the film's director, Michael Mann. Pulling onto the studio lot, a rush of adrenaline fired through my stomach. The sun was high in the sky that day, not a cloud to be seen. I smelled the freshly cut lawn surrounding the lot. The birds chirped in the distance. I felt at once alive and at peace. I wasn't thinking of my past hurt and pain, but rather the hope and optimism of finding what might be my true calling: leading others to extended greatness.

I walked into the building, where the receptionist greeted me and escorted me to the boardroom. The freshly waxed marble tile floors of the hallway reminded me of the University of Maryland library. I took in the table in the center of the room, a dark mahogany behemoth, twelve-feet long and five-feet wide, with a glossy shellac coating. The chairs surrounding the table were genuine black leather, the look of pure luxury. The recessed lights of the ceiling reflected in the table's sheen, providing a comfortable vibe for the occasion. Several studio executives politely greeted me and we quickly moved to the matter at hand.

Sitting across the table from Michael Mann, I was able to look him directly in the face and tell him about my expertise and experience in the field of training, coaching, and bringing champions to world titles. It was not about me convincing him that I was qualified for this job; it was just the universe illuminating his world to the fact that I had already been chosen for this task.

Michael Mann told me he wanted to set up an audition with Will Smith. I asked him who was the one auditioning who, and he said, "We need to see if Will likes you." I responded, "I already know how to fight. We need to see if I like him." The room erupted in laughter, but my face didn't move. I was too serious. I was trying to change the world.

A few days later, Will and I met for a training session at the 18th Street Gym in Santa Monica, California, a hidden gym in the basement of a Jewish temple owned by singer Bob Dylan. After a quick hello, I told Will, "Put those gloves on. We are boxing." Without hesitation, he gloved up and we trained. For a solid two hours, I treated him like he was a fighter, not an actor.

After the workout, the studio's production representative told me, "We're interviewing other people, so we will let you know." But I felt great about meeting Will in the ring and felt that the call would come much sooner than later.

Ten minutes after leaving that training session, I received a call from the studio. The job was mine. Although I was mentally prepared for this news, I couldn't help being as excited as I'd ever been. I immediately called Piano to tell her the news. As we chatted, I felt an overwhelming sense of joy as I realized what an honor it would be to work on this film.

Not too long thereafter, I found out that Will had turned down the role of Ali multiple times, and it wasn't until I was chosen to choreograph the fights and train him that he agreed to do the film. He instinctively knew I was the guy who would get him to where he needed to be and to go beyond what anyone ever dreamed he could be as a fighter.

I prepared extensively for this job, expanding my skill set to include the detailed intricacies of lighting and cameras, and what it takes to combine real professional fighting with motion picture choreography. Michael Mann did not want this to be picture or stunt fighting—he wanted real hitting. Special gloves were designed to limit the impact of blows so that actors could really hit one another in the fight scenes. This wasn't just about the fighting for me. It was about properly preparing myself to carry out the biggest task of my lifetime.

14

TRANSFORMATION

Right away, Will and I met to discuss our vision for the direction of the film.

He knew this was a career-defining role for him and was committed to excellence not only as an actor, but as a fighter. I agreed that I would give everything I had. All I asked in return was that he follow my lead and stay focused on becoming a world class fighter.

To be a professional fighter, you must have a firm foundation of supreme physicality and conditioning. The body has to be primed for the extensive cardiovascular stress that happens in the ring. By February, Will and I had been training on his physicality and conditioning for three months. He was in the best shape of his life, and now it was time to master the boxing. I'd been training him as if he were an amateur fighter, teaching him the fundamentals: balance, defense, and footwork. We hadn't approached Ali's style of fighting yet. It was still about learning how to box, instilling into Will a fighter's instinct. In our heated sparring sessions, I tried to convey the true essence of fear in the ring, so he could know how it felt when someone was standing on the other side of the ring, ready to take his head off—for real.

I'd brought Will to a point of no return. He'd managed to withstand the pressures and kept going, but it couldn't stop there. When he could no longer stand due to exhaustion, it was vital that he understand what it felt like to have the wind knocked out of him during the 13th round and have his friends and family screaming, "Get up Champ!" It would take a superhuman resolve and commitment to a greater purpose, so I was transforming Will into a fighter both in and out of the ring. Will had to understand that it is was this kind of commitment and dedication to the cause that creates champions. Yes, he was one of the most successful music and film star in the world, but we had to push beyond that. We had to raise the bar, because this picture had to elevate people not just when it hit theaters, but for many years to come, as this would represent Ali's life and legacy.

With the boxing, Will was trying hard, but it hadn't fully clicked for him yet, and I knew I was going to have to put even more pressure on him. For instance, he needed to get away from using that over-protective nose guard and all that gear. This wasn't for wimps. It was time for him to let go of the side of pool. I couldn't let him get hurt, but I had to somehow to teach him to become the real deal. I owed it to Ali. I thought, I'm going to bring him along. He's my fighter. I like him a lot. He's got heart, and boxing is 90% heart. It's up to me to help him shock the world.

Months had passed before we dived into the Muhammad Ali style of boxing. We finally started working on the great Ali's basic styles and idiosyncrasies, the most important one being his ability to make other fighters miss. I taught Will how to judge distance and control the space between him and his opponent. Ali could appear to be in range for his opponent to strike, but when the attack was executed, he wasn't there to be hit—that's what you call ring generalship. You have to create a mental and physical illusion through your footwork. You are leaning, constantly moving and using your angles. The opponent is like a train on a railroad track; all you need to do is dance to one side of the track and the only way the train can hit you is if it derails itself. Will came to understand that the train (the opponent) had to derail itself (be off-balance) because the optimal time to punch and strike an opponent is in that moment. This strategy sounds simple in theory, but it's difficult in practice because the fighter has to always be one second ahead of the opponent's fist.

I also taught Will Ali's signature punches, punches that were the essence of his offensive style. The left jab and the overhand right were the big ones, but there were so many more. For instance, Ali had nine different jabs. One he called the "snake lick," a punch that came from the floor—

really down low— it can be compared to a cobra striking. There's also Ali's rapid-fire jab: three to five jabs thrown in succession at his opponent's eyes. If done correctly, it would create a blur in the boxer's face so he wouldn't be able to see Ali's hard right hand coming behind it.

Thanks to our heated sparring sessions, Will developed an understanding of how elusive Ali was. He understood why he had to be like that when he had fighters such as Joe Frazier and George Foreman trying to knock off his head. Will had a visceral experience that helped him truly understand Ali.

I even taught him how to stand when he was in public, since fighters have a different way of carrying themselves. The strength and confidence that comes from learning to fight and protect yourself doesn't just stay in the ring. It's amplified by everyday life. Fighters stand a little taller, a little straighter, and seem to have a slight edge of arrogance about them. They know that if a confrontation were to break out, they wouldn't be the one running for the door. They have the skills and competence to fight back, to protect themselves and the others around them.

I was training Will as a professional fighter heading towards a world title bout, careful not to peak too soon—because after the peak, it's all downhill. When you're at the top of Mt. Everest, the only steps are down. After ten months, Will truly understood the principles and methods that I had been teaching him. He hit the peak at the right point, right when we were ready to film the first fight scene of the movie.

I shouldn't have been surprised that being back in the ring brought up raw feelings of rage and turmoil, but I knew I couldn't let the Monster resurface and destroy me. I had made it this far. I would keep pressing. After much encouragement from Piano, I kept a journal during my work on the Ali project. I had never wanted to write before because I didn't want to remember my life's painful memories, but I made a commitment to keep account of this experience.

For instance, on August 13th, 2000, I wrote: "I realize now it truly is all about the Journey. I thank God for blessing me with the suffering and tribulation, because it's all these experiences that are necessary to see life's secrets. 'Many Are Called & Few Are Chosen.' Only through my own pain can my mind and heart be open to see the significance of Ali's journey and to guide Will to the level of insight to have the ability to show the world Ali's story."

I was also responsible for helping cast the appropriate fighters to play Ali's opponents. Current World Champion fighters were hired to portray former World Champion fighters to create a feeling of authenticity in the ring. Michael Bent played Sonny Liston. James Toney played Joe Frazier. Alfred Cole played Ernie Terrell. Charles Shufford played George Foreman. Robert Sale played Jerry Quarry. Vincent Cook played Jimmy Ellis. And Damien "Bolo" Wills played Ken Norton.

There were a total of twelve fights that would appear in the film and I was in charge of choreographing all of them. There would be no old footage used for this movie, so every single fight had to be re-created, even the fights that appeared on TV screens in the background. This was a grueling process, and I spent hours pacing my living room, trying to figure out how to pull it off. I knew I had to turn a current World Champion who'd won world titles fighting one way into a World Champion from years past fighting a completely different way. Also, I had to design something that would help them understand different, and, sometimes, diametrically opposed, fighting styles. Plus, I had to devise a way for the fighters to remember the specific sequence of punches for each fight.

After hours of planning and plotting, it hit me: numbers. I would assign a number to each particular punch, creating a simple yet effective punching system for all of the fight scenes. Just like the actors had to learn lines for their scenes, every actor, sparring partner, and professional training fighter had to learn these codes.

During training, I called out a series of numbers representing different punches and the fighters had to perform the punch sequences to perfection. Since we were recreating real boxing bouts, we could leave no room for error. The fights had to be exact. The codes for each punch I used during my training regimen were:

1= Left Jab

2 = Straight Right Hand

3 = Left Hook to the Head

4 = Right Hook to the Body

5 = Left Hook to the Body

6 = Right Uppercut

7 = Left Uppercut

8 = Right Hook to the Head

I developed a world class system that would create a one-of-a-kind realism in the ring for this movie, but these men were beasts, pit bulls, trained fighting dogs, ready to devour, and Will Smith was the raw meat. They asked, "What you want us to do with the kid?"

I said, "If you hurt him, give him a minute to get his head together. If he goes down, don't kick him."

Day in and day out, it was war, a gym full of testosterone and rage. These professional fighters in all weight divisions had the same rage and pain that I had inside of me. They were all fighting their inner demons, snapping into lethal weapons inside the ring, and keeping charge was my duty. Although every man in the room was larger than me, I knew it was no accident I was their leader. I had fought a giant those many years ago so I could grow up and teach giants the lessons of the world. But I also became the protector of the lamb. I was the guide. The coach.

Ali himself even came to the gym and saw some of the work we were doing for the film. I'd first met him when I was a teenager, around the time I won the Golden Gloves, and we'd crossed paths many times in my professional career since he was around a lot of Sugar Ray Leonard fights (he admired Sugar Ray's style because it was a lot like his own). Ali stood by the ring and watched as Will emulated his style, throwing punches with me in the center of the ring. At one point, Ali fixed me with that look of his and said, "You are doing an amazing job." For all the times I hadn't been recognized for my gifts and skills, for all the times I wanted to escape, for all the times I took the pain on the chin—this moment made it worth it. His words resonated deep in my heart and made me proud of how far I'd come and what I was able to do despite my rough beginnings. That was a life changing moment.

After completing principal photography of Round 1, the first fight in the film, I wrote in my journal: "January 12, 2001, Extreme intensity with the fight action. Will is on point. He is Ali. His timing is great–fifty years from now this will be the history marker for the life of Ali."

I couldn't have been more proud of the transition that Will had made into Ali. We made a great team. Just after completing the Frazier fights, I wrote in my journal: "February 6, 2001, Frazier I & II completed. Eight fights in the can. Excellent fight footage (best ever done for film.) Will *is* Ali–his skills improve every day!"

The production took us all over the world, and we spent a great deal of time in Africa, where we were warmly welcomed by the indigenous people of Mozambique. A truly beautiful place, it reminded me of my roots. There, I felt a real pride for my ancestry. I had come quite a distance from the abused little boy who was told he wouldn't amount to anything in life, but it was all made possible because of the will and intestinal fortitude of the black men and women who sacrificed their lives so that I could be here today.

When Will and I ran the dirt paths of Mozambique, I never felt more free. The people of the tribes would sometime run after us, chanting, "Ali, Ali, Ali," because, in their minds, Will *was* Ali. These profound experiences made me exceptionally proud of my fighter.

There is nobody who worked harder, who put in longer hours, or took this job more personally than I did. I even broke my hand while training the fighters for this movie when I accidentally hit Robert Sale's elbow with a hard right hand. It was a freak accident, something that should have never happened in a hundred years, but it didn't stop me from working. With a fist shaped cast on my hand, I was in the ring every single day, making sure that every second of fighting captured on film was accurate and exact. Nothing would get in the way of me fulfilling what I had come to believe as my greater calling. It was an honor to work on this project, for the sake of what Ali meant to me and to the world.

There was nobody there to tell me what to do or how to do it. I just did it, and I knew I'd found my calling. It came to me like magic. I was in my world. It was what I was great at. I loved it. It was visceral to me. I was in the zone, the space where freedom to create brings you close to the Creator. I had won. I was finally free from the abuse, the suffering, and all the wrongdoings. My frat brothers back east and my family were all proud of the fact that I was making such a significant contribution to the world. Things made sense, and I was at peace about what I had been through and who I had become. It was a wonderful time.

However, little did I know that the biggest battle of my life was yet to come.

15

THE THING THAT ALMOST BROKE ME

Ali was going to be the Christmas blockbuster of 2001, so even before the movie hit theaters there was press everywhere.

Everyone was talking about this film: would Will be able to accurately portray Ali? Would this be an Oscar contender? Magazines, newspapers, nightly news channels, gossip columns, billboards, buzz on the street—it was all about *Ali*, and I couldn't have been more proud. Piano and my frat brothers—Sam, Jose, Stan, and, of course, Ray—all knew how invested I'd been in this project and were thrilled to see that I'd made it. I finally did something good that everybody could appreciate. There were plenty of people who doubted us, but I knew Will would shock the world.

That Spring, about eight months before the film's release, I received a call from Forward Pass Productions, Michael Mann's production company. The caller hesitantly introduced himself as one of the PR representatives working on Ali. A few quick niceties later, he told me something that immediately took my breath away: Angelo Dundee would get credit for training Will Smith to play Muhammad Ali.

Angelo Dundee was Muhammad Ali's corner man for all but two of his professional fights throughout his career. He had trained him in the fighter's early days as Cassius Clay and followed him through his world titles and accomplishments as the G.O.A.T. (Greatest of All Time). There was no question that Angelo Dundee was the one responsible for training Muhammad Ali, but in no way was he the man who stepped back into the ring and transformed Will Smith into Ali for this film. Yes, Angelo Dundee had joined us for a few weeks, but no way in hell was he responsible for Will's transformation. This was me, and me alone! I was the one who got beat up on for hours each day. I was the one who ran twenty-five miles a week with Will. I was the one who sacrificed myself for the good of this film.

How could they deny me?

After taking a moment to digest the news, a bit confused, I roared, "*What?*"

He calmly repeated the news and explained that an official letter had been mailed out, but that he'd wanted me to hear it firsthand from the production office, to prevent any confusion.

This PR flack proceeded to explain that making and marketing a Hollywood movie required that a complex set of tools work together to design an efficient (read: money-making) machine. All marketing campaigns are designed to sell tickets, and these campaigns sometimes have to tweak the reality of what happened behind the scenes—it's an industry thing—so the studio had decided that, in the best interest of the marketing for this film, Angelo Dundee would get credit for training Will Smith to play Muhammad Ali.

What the fuck? Hell no!

Piano immediately recognized that something was awfully wrong. She mouthed, "What's wrong?" I know she saw my eyes turn bloodshot, and she realized that whatever news I had just received had infuriated me beyond anything that she'd ever seen before in our five-year relationship. Just when I thought I had conquered the demon, here he was again. But life had made me hard. I'd built impenetrable steel walls to protect myself. However, I'd made a choice to expose my soul for the purpose of this project, and this hurt. And when it hurts, I don't get sad—I get mad.

After I hung up the phone, my blood pressure shot through the roof. My heart rate accelerated, the adrenaline crashed through my body like a tsunami, and I snapped. With every ounce of my strength, I hurled the silver cordless phone across the room, where it hit the wall and shattered into pieces. I roared at the top of my lungs. In that moment, I wanted to kill someone.

After such betrayal, I was no longer the Darrell who had come so far in the world. Instead, I was again the little boy who still hurt from the pain and injustice of his childhood, the person who vowed to never feel again, to never let anyone come emotionally close. The rage that welled up in my being was unexplainable and unfathomable. I was a savage wild dog foaming at the mouth, ready to maul anything and everything in my path. I was enraged at the production team, furious at the industry, and mostly angry with myself. I felt like a sucka! I fell for the hype. I put in every morsel of passion I had, only to be rejected—again. I couldn't take the pain. I was tired of fighting a losing battle. At that moment, I regretted going back to boxing.

I was reminded of *The Ten Commandments*, the film my father had taken me to all those years ago, and of Moses being denied entrance into the Promised Land after leading the people out of Egypt. He had sacrificed days, weeks, months, years, walking across the scorching heat of the desert, somehow surviving with little water and on mere morsels of bread. He battled the powers of Egypt who refused to free the people, boldly pursuing that which he believed. Freeing the people and holding the mighty hand of God in his staff, he parted the Red Sea to bring God's people out of bondage. Retreating to the dangers of Mt. Sinai, Moses faced the fears of death and saw again the face of God and witnessed the fire of His Word being etched into the tablets of Law. He was responsible not only for freeing the people, but also for bringing order to the chaos and saving God's people from their sinful ways.

At the point in which Moses could enter the Promised Land, the land of milk and honey, where he would receive freedom and rest from the trials of his journey, he was denied entrance. I know now why my father chose that movie for me so many years ago. I understood that personal sacrifice for the greater good of man was a necessity on my path to greatness.

At this point, it was just me and my shadow. I had a choice to make: I could destroy it all, or I could once again take the pain on the chin. I knew I'd given the project my all—Will had morphed into Ali, and his role would ultimately earn him an Academy Award nomination, the first of his career—and there was nothing more left to give. I felt a righteous and rightful anger at the studio's wrongdoings, and my rage would not subside until I exacted my revenge. If they wouldn't willingly give me credit for my work on the film, I was going to take it. I felt like going up to the studio lot and snatching one of those damn executives out of his chair and leaving everything I had fought for in my life, right there on the pavement. I would not go down without a fight.

16

PERSPECTIVE

In his song, "Beautiful Boy," John Lennon sings, "Life is what happens to you while you are busy making other plans," and I would soon learn exactly what he meant.

Although the phone call from that PR flack ripped everything I worked so hard to achieve from my hands, I soon received a call that sent me into the darkest abyss. Let me backtrack:

In 1977, when I was twenty years old, I fathered a beautiful little girl named Keeana. When she came home from the hospital, I was confined to a wheelchair due to an accident at work when my foot was run over and I partially lost one of my toes. I would hold Keeana in my arms and ride her around in my wheelchair. She was a beautiful angel and I was so proud to be her pops. I'd always heard about the unconditional love parents have for their children—and it was then that I finally understood it. It was my first experience as a parent and I vowed to be the best father any man could be. I understood what it was to look to a parent to offer love and cuddles and all the stuff that parents were supposed to provide. I didn't receive it, so it was that much more important that I provide it for my kids.

I spent a lot of time with her as a child—ironing her dresses, braiding her hair, reading her stories. I would ask her, "Who am I?" and with a big smile she would say, "Macaroni." Then I would ask her, "Who are you?"

and she would say "Cheese," then burst into laughter. So we became Mac and Cheese. It touched the depths of my soul to have such a special bond with this little girl. I would tell her that I loved her and it was so special to watch as her eyes lit up and, with her sweet little voice, try to make out the words, *I love you too.*

Simply put, she was Daddy's little girl.

Her mother and I soon split up due to the substance abuse she had been struggling with for so long. Keeana ended up being close to her mother: they were more like sisters than they were mother and daughter. They hung out and partied together. It wasn't the relationship that a child needs with a mother.

Sadly, Keeana's mother died of drug related AIDS and, as she dealt with the loss of her mother—who was also her best friend—Keeana fell into a deep depression. She then turned to drug and substance abuse herself. Our relationship became estranged because I would not tolerate this type of lifestyle.

I called Keeana on her nineteenth birthday. I heard in her voice that she was lost, searching for her place in the world. Unfortunately, she continued to find solace in substances. I knew this way of life would only lead her to destruction. I made a choice to harshly instruct her about the pitfalls of such a lifestyle, and while she heard my voice, she never truly heard my message.

In the fall of 2001, right after the Ali mess, I learned that my firstborn daughter, my angel, my little Mac and Cheese, had senselessly ended her life by climbing into a bathtub, placing a nine-millimeter into her mouth, pulling the trigger, and blowing her brains out.

My little girl was gone. My body cramped in pain, my bowels shifted violently, and I threw up every morsel of food in my stomach with brutal force. My throat swelled up, constricting my airway, making it almost impossible to breathe. My thoughts spun ferociously out of control. I lost my footing. I was upside-down as my knees buckled and my body fell to the ground. I died inside. Everything in me was ripped out, chewed up, and destroyed. I lost it. Pain has no name; it has no identity. Hurts can linger forever and there are no words to explain the gut wrenching pain that took over me. My wife saw me cry for the first time that night. The agony was so excruciating that the next forty-eight hours was a fog of reality. Not only did all the colors disappear, but my world disappeared. I was in an absolute void. I had no emotions, no feelings, no thoughts. Nothing.

I died that night. I was a walking dead man.

My son, Darrell Foster, Jr., was born a couple of years after Keeana and had had a tight relationship with his sister. He held me responsible for Keeana's death. He didn't want to talk to me at all, even though, when he was a child, Darrell and I had been inseparable. I called Darrell "Pacman," and it was always me and Pacman, Pacman and me. I was devastated by being rejected by my son, but I was so numb to hurt and pain at this point that it could've been worse, I suppose. Getting hit over and over causes you to lose feeling in the body and, as in my case, the mind. It killed me inside to think that I could have been the one to save my daughter. Then, to have my son reject me —well, I just didn't want to feel a thing.

I fell into a deep depression of my own, blocking out the pain and memories and regrets and all the things that could have or should have been. I thought the world was unfair when I got the Ali phone call, but now I was suicidal in a lonely, dark, tragic, dismal world.

I still don't know how I survived, and I truly wish I did, because it's something I could use to help other people. But I slowly started picking up the pieces and putting myself back together. I went back to the things that offered me comfort in times of despair: my reading and my running.

Fueled by anger, hurt and pain, I'd always chosen to push relentlessly toward success, but Keeana's death tragically revealed to me that life is not about those things. It became so clear to me that I'd let rage and anger blind me to how a human being should live, that life is not individual successes and riches, cars, houses, money, and material wealth. It is about friends and family and serving mankind.

I asked myself, *Have I been worthy of my suffering? Have I?* I knew that I had not spent my life in service of others. For the most part, my life had been only about me. I had not made a concerted effort to help other people and share in their stories. I had been so caught up in my own tragedies and what I didn't have as a child that I forgot about others in the process, even close friends and family.

Remembering what saved me as a child, I picked up books that I had long forgotten about and was reminded about the truths that ancient wisdom had laid out before me as clues for my journey. I started training my brain and my body again, but not for my own success. I now realized that my life was meant for someone else: for you. I understood that I had to suffer so that others could find their path in life. I had a duty. After all, my suffering had to be for a bigger purpose.

Life is about choices, and often times we don't get a second chance. I would not have another opportunity to do things differently in the past, but I did have a choice in the present, which would greatly affect my future. This made me reflect on my life, not to ask why, but to realize that I've been given these experiences of my lifetime so that the world may be taught the lessons and so that other people may learn from me and go on to achieve great things. Who was I to keep bitching and whining? There is no pain greater than losing a child, and the only way that I could know peace was to remind myself of the greater calling in my life, that I was meant to be a coach, a mentor, and a sage for those that followed after me. (In time, I reconciled and restored my relationship with my son, Darrell. Although still miles apart, with his home in Maryland and mine in Los Angeles, our bond became stronger than ever.)

All of this happened within a few short months and I was forced to face the Ali project again as the release date was soon approaching. Just weeks before the release of the movie, my son called me on the phone and said, "Pops, I thought you trained Will for Ali. The magazine says Angelo Dundee trained him."

I could have made the choice to get angry again, but by this point I had decided the issue was small in comparison to my ultimate duty to mankind. My destiny would not hang on the hinges of a movie. I had to keep pressing, keep pursing my greater calling. My work on Ali wasn't the final duty for me. I still had work to do. I had to help other people find their passions through the perspective I had gained from my recent awakening and the lessons I had learned along the way.

I went to Will to tell him about the controversy and he said that, despite what the studio had to say, he would tell the world that I had been the one who had trained him. As a guest on Oprah Winfrey's show, he told the studio audience and the millions of viewers at home that I was, in fact, his trainer. The truth eventually made its way to newsstands and media outlets, and my months of hard work and dedication were vindicated.

Although having a tangible acknowledgement of my work was gratifying, it truly wasn't about the credit. I was thankful that the truth was made known, but as I started to my resurrection and journey as a new man, my perspective changed to that of someone who understood the greater calling placed upon me. It wasn't until I walked through the fire of my lifetime, suffered great pain, great hardships, rejection, and even greater loss, that I was able to clearly see what had been divinely orchestrated for my life. I knew that the things I learned would benefit others and that's when I knew I would be a coach for many more people to come.

Since working with Will Smith on *Ali*, I have created a personal bond with him as confidant and friend. We are actually more than friends: we are family. He stood up for me when everyone else turned their backs. Even today we work together and train our intellect and anatomies as we continue to give back to the world through our unique talents.

Over the years, in addition to working with people who want to get in the best shape of their lives, I've trained, coached and mentored numerous celebrities, such as Jada Pinkett-Smith, Tisha Campbell-Martin, Forest Whitaker, Mykelti Williamson, Terrence Howard, Nick Cannon, Blair Underwood, Virginia Madsen, Alice Braga, Jason Clarke, Molly Allen, Spencer Breslin, Lolita Davidovich, Duane Martin, Caleeb Pinkett, Bridget Moynahan, Eddie Murphy, Kevin Phillips, Tyrese Gibson, Ana de la Reguera, Angelica Russo, Ving Rhames, Gabriele Muccino, Chico Benymon, Darren Shahlavi, Michael Bentt, James Tony, Ice Cole, James Shuford, Mario Van Pebbles, Blake Lirette, Pete "Sugarfoot" Cunningham, and Steve Tisch. Much of the training that I do with my clients happens between the ears. I am able to step into their world, meet them at the place on their journey, and offer the tools that they need to achieve the next step.

I don't differentiate or categorize those whose path I cross because I believe that we all exist for a unique purpose. The most elite people in the world come to me for my experience and expertise. I have the highest possible standards in the world and, if you trust in yourself, I promise we will make it to whatever it is that you wish to accomplish. I will never ask you to do something that I won't do with you. I live by the words in the poem "Sermons We See" by Edgar Guest, which says: "I know you would rather see a sermon than to hear one any day. I know you would rather watch what I do than to listen to what I say."

My reformation into a man who can understand my past and live in a moment of present gratitude with perspective of a better future did not come easy. And while it has taken years to craft together the meaning of things into a concise offering, I realized that this part of my journey has really just begun as I share life with my two young children, Giovanni and

Bella.

It was January 17, 2011, Martin Luther King Day. I was sitting in the dining room of my home with my one-year-old daughter, Bella, and my three-year-old son, Giovanni. These people are angels. When I look into their eyes, I see hope for the future and a better tomorrow. I thank God that I was blessed with such a wonderful family and I'm making sure to give my children the love and the guidance that I had never had as a little boy.

While I was busy instructing my children on the ways of the world and what it takes to survive, I got an unexpected lesson of my own that day. Giovanni is the most brilliant little person that I've ever met. He is far beyond his years in understanding the complexities of life. His mother always tells me there's something special about him, and while I believe her, I am aware that both of us may be a little biased. However, while eating dinner as a family that night, Giovanni put down his pizza, looked at me with his big brown eyes, and said, "Papa, what have you done to change the world?"

Out of the mouth of babes, I thought. Children are so quick to illuminate truth.

The profound nature of his question coupled with the innocence of his tone changed the molecules in the room. A rush went through my body as the universe reached down and tapped me on the shoulder. I wanted tell him, "Well, I brought you into this world," but I knew that was not a good enough answer, that it would be a cop-out. In a blur, my life passed before my eyes in a series of picture flashcards with the last card featuring the phrase, *What have you done to change the world?*

I didn't have a speech prepared to answer my son—I could only speak the truth straight from my heart. I thought of all the slaves, the men, women, and children, who died so I could be free and all the sacrifices made by great leaders before me, all so I could have the life that I have today. I paused, then looked at Piano and said, "You're right. He is special." After a minute of thought, I told Giovanni that, in life, we are always responsible for giving back. We have a duty to touch the lives of other people in extraordinary ways, and there's a greater calling for us all, that our journeys are not over until they're over, and it's only then that everything begins. He, as well as all of us, have a responsibility to empower others. I further explained that, as a child who has everything, it was now his job to make his friend's lives better. That's his job, and we all, no matter our age or vocation, have that very same job.

Giovanni's name means "God is Gracious" and Bella's means "Beautiful Sanctuary." I am humbled to be called their father. I am a better person now. I allow myself to take in beautiful memories and appreciate the important moments in life. When I come home from work, my kids run to me with open arms, exclaiming "Papa! You're home!" They will never understand the scars on the inside of my soul or the tears that I hold hostage in my heart from pain or what I went through to survive to this day, but what they do understand is the love that I express when I wrap my arms around them, tell them I love them, and just *breathe*.

EPILOGUE

Despite our upbringings or the unfortunate circumstances that we may have had to face in life, we are all ordinary people who have the opportunity to do extraordinary things.

Life is about choices, and we see one of the greatest examples of choices and honest introspection in the story of the "The Lady or the Tiger," written in 1882 by Frank R. Stockton. The story goes like this:

In days past, a barbaric king devised a unique system of justice. When an offense came against the king, the offender was placed into an arena with two doors. Behind one door was a ferocious lion who would immediately and effortlessly devour the man. Behind the other door was a beautiful princess who the man would immediately call his wife.

The king received word that a young man of meager means fell in love with his daughter and she with him. The man was forced into the arena where he must choose a door. The princess behind the door was not the king's daughter, rather some other woman. The daughter, who loved the man greatly, found out what was behind each of the doors that her lover would be faced with in the arena. When the young man looked up at her, she pointed to the right door, signaling this was the best choice for him.

Therein lies the dilemma. If she pointed to the door with the princess, she would lose her love. These people, being barbarians, lacked selflessness, so it wouldn't be beyond the princess to choose death for her lover rather than to give him to another woman. Here's the choice: the young man must decide what he believes to be behind the right door, the lady or the tiger?

When asked for the solution, Stockton replied, "If you decided which it is—the lady or the tiger—you find out what kind of person you are yourself." Your choice is dictated upon how you see the world and how you view mankind.

No matter where you are in this life, no matter where you aspire to be, you have a choice in the matter. Take a deep breath and consider these questions, "Does your shadow match your shape? Are you who you say you are?" At the end of the day, you have to look at yourself in the mirror and be okay with who you see.

It's my responsibility to share with you the secrets and the message of my life. Illumination of truth must always be our goal. So, regardless of your excuse or what you may say in rebuttal, this is for you. The only way to make it through hard times and still achieve your aspirations is to understand that your body is a holy vessel. You must continually train your intellect and your anatomy.

Challenge yourself to think outside of your own limited reality. Allow yourself to be open enough to know how to see and to know how to know. Read, read, and read some more. Ignorance is never an excuse. Allow your mind to be a sponge for information and never let an opportunity slide past because you weren't prepared to see it.

This life is not a sprint. It's a marathon. It's about endurance. When training for world titles, the start is always exhilarating. Everyone is supportive. The team is all running behind you. The press is everywhere to capture the moment for the world to see. But then comes the middle. The middle of the journey is lonely. It always—without fail—gets more difficult. And this is where true passion comes in.

When I train with people all over the world, it's mandatory they run five miles. If they are physically able to run, it's not an option. No matter if they've never run before, if they despise the act of running, and most importantly if they say they just "can't run." This practice reveals the true nature of what they want. Many tell me, "I want to be the best in the world at _____." You fill in the blank. What the tangible goal is doesn't really matter. If you want something, anything, bad enough, you will do whatever it takes to get it.

The five-mile run is the representation of internal journey we must all travel on the path toward our outward goals and aspirations. Mile one is exciting. You are on the treadmill (or on the beach or the road or the dirt path) and you stand proud at the commitment to begin. You take a mental picture of yourself, posture perfect, back straight, chest open, arms moving in sync with your stride. You feel the air on your face and notice the surroundings, as the world looks a little more alive than when you woke up that morning.

Mile five is exciting, but for much different reasons. You can see the light at the end of the tunnel. The closer you get to your goal, the easier it is to keep pursuing it. This is the importance of keeping track of your dreams and noting the progress along the way.

In the five-mile run, the true test of our willingness to pay the price and, more importantly, the true test of our intestinal fortitude comes between mile one and mile five. Your breathing becomes labored. Your eyesight is not so clear anymore. You start contemplating the act of stopping. Your stomach hurts. Your toes are blistering. Your hip flexors are aching. Your calves are cramping. Your legs are on fire. What you do between mile one and mile five is what truly matters. It's not fun. It hurts. It's hard. And those people who were with you at the beginning are nowhere to be found. You are alone. Do you really want what you say you want? Or are you just paying lip service to it? Your body is a living, breathing organism that must be challenged and trained.

There's a secret to an elevated existence. When your body is functioning at prime potential, you view the world through clearer lenses. Obstacles become small hurdles and you began to realize that there's not anything you can't accomplish. I know through my years of experience and expertise that this is what it takes to succeed. There are no magic pills, potions, or spells. The secret lies *within you.*

Kevin Hall, in his book, *Aspire: Discovering Your Passion Through the Power of Words*, writes, "Being a leader means finding the path. But before you can help someone else find their path, you must know yours." Honest introspective will illuminate the abilities that you have been given so that you may give back to the world. You have to learn who you are and follow that. Nobody can figure it out for you. You have to see it and acknowledge it in yourself. Claim your potential for greatness and don't allow your past to get in your way.

Remember that in the quest for an answer to the question, "What makes us human?" We cannot overlook the past, for the past is a story that has been written to provide light for the path of today. Great men and women, leaders from all walks of life, have committed to digging in the trenches to unearth the truths that make up our present reality. You have to be willing to dig, to excavate, to unleash the pain, the hurts, the unjust deeds, the unfair acts and the intolerable wrongdoings of the past so that you may learn from them and progress forward. Always keep it moving and seek out the keys to knowledge and wisdom that unravel the scrolls placed here for us throughout time.

In *The Republic*, Plato outlined a timeless scenario in which we should model our lives. In this story, we find a cave of prisoners who have been chained to the ground and chained by their heads to the walls of the cave since childhood. They can only see the wall of the cave in front of them. Behind them is a walkway where people walk, talk, and carry objects, including figures of men and animals made of wood, stone, and other materials. The shadows of the activity taking place behind the prisoners are reflected onto the cave walls by light of fire that burns behind the walkway. The prisoners perceive the shadows and echoes of the talk as reality.

Upon release from the chains, the fire, the objects, and the people in the walkway frighten the freed prisoner. When he is told that the people and things he now perceives are more real than the shadows, at first he will not believe. He will want to return to his old perceptions, viewing shadows as reality.

Being dragged out of the cave and into the world of day, the power of the sun will be blinding to him. However, he will gradually see the stars and the moon and then see the shadows in the daylight, created by the sun. He will see objects in the full light of day, creating a new reality. The sun makes this new perception possible. If the prisoner returns to the Cave and his old world, he will not be able to function well in his old world of shadows, for he has already seen the truth of the light. Sharing with his old fellows, his newfound truth will be rejected by those who are still chained to the wall, imprisoned in their world of false reality.

Knowing the truth does not just stop with knowledge for oneself. It has been given for a reason. Regardless of the hesitation, the refusal and rebuke, it is the freed prisoner's responsibility to return to the Cave to rescue his friends. And likewise, if life has blessed us with lessons of truths, it is our responsibility to return and save the people we care about as well.

Life is not about what could have been or what we were going to do. Life is about living. It's about discovering your passion and making a decision that "if you want something in life, go get it. Period."

I strive to be a Warrior, a philosopher, a leader amongst men, a pathfinder who has sought all my life the great wisdoms and truths of ancient times, eastern mysticism, and western philosophy. All leaders of life— Jesus, Gandhi, Buddha, Prometheus—proved that bringing a great message to the world comes with sacrifice and great cost. My task to suffer and survive, finding the breadcrumbs and clues to life's complex riddles, was for you. I've researched the world, traveled the world and been on journeys throughout time and space all to bring this message of hope and inspiration. If I can make it, you can too.

I look to the sky for my star, for my guiding light. Reflecting back on the day that my star discovered me, I understand that it wasn't just a bullshit, unfortunate life, but all for a grander purpose. I've sought to do great things like other great men, but I still wonder, *Have I suffered enough? Am I worthy?*

There was definitely a turning point when I realized that I had to go in with the truth of my life and my stories for the purpose of this book and how that would touch lives around the world and thus make the world a better place. Perhaps you question what your own legacy will be. What have you done, or what will you do, for the next generation? What profound, honest, compassionate thing have you done or could you do for your fellow man?

I ran from my calling, but it never left me. It's no coincidence that it was the boxing and fighting I used to escape and survive that ended up being my legacy. I am not a great artist or great pianist or a great singer or a dancer—but maybe you are. I am not scientifically or mechanically inclined and, honestly, I hate putting things together—but maybe you love it. Whatever it is about you that makes you *you*, it's your responsibility to identify it and then do something worthwhile about it.

My passion and love for living, and, ultimately, greater success, is what allowed me to endure the situations of my lifetime. Victor Frankl endured the harshest of human suffering in the German concentration camps of World War II. For three years, Frankl suffered the most absurd, painful, dehumanizing situations, yet chose to rise above and discover meaning from such horrific events. In his book, *Man's Search for Meaning*, Frankl not only recounts the dark experiences as a prisoner of war, but moves to an elevated realm of existence where he makes sense out of his suffering, understanding that it was endured for the greater good of mankind. He wrote, "It did not really matter what we expected from life, but rather what life expected from us. We needed to stop asking about the meaning of life, and instead to think of ourselves as those who were being questioned by life—daily and hourly. Our answer must consist not in talk and meditation, but in right action and in right conduct. Life ultimately means taking the responsibility to find the right answer to its problems and to fulfill the tasks which it constantly sets for each individual."

Viktor Frankl was passionate about life. He allowed his experiences to strengthen his will to survive and to leave the world a better place. His story has no ending, for his life, which started in 1905, and his legacy, marked by death in 1997, has only just begun: "Our core drive as humans is our search for meaning. The way in which a man accepts his fate and all the sufferings that it entails, the way in which he takes up his cross, gives him ample opportunity—even under the most difficult circumstances—to add a deeper meaning to his life."

I will leave you with one of the most powerful stories about the truth about all of us, the truth of human nature, contained in this story of Brahma:

According to an old Hindu legend, there was a time when all men and women were gods, but they so abused their divinity that Brahma, the chief god, decided to take it away from men and women and hide it where they would never again find it. Where to hide it became the big question.

When the lesser gods were called in council to consider this question, they said, "We will bury man's divinity deep in the earth." But Brahma said, "No, that will not do, for man will dig deep down into the earth and find it."

Then they said, "We will sink his divinity into the deepest ocean." But again Brahma replied, "No, not out there, for man will learn to devise a way to dive into the deepest waters, will search out the ocean bed, and will find it."

Then the lesser gods said, "We will take it to the top of the mountain and there hide it." But again Brahma replied, "No, for man will eventually climb every high mountain on earth. He will be sure some day to find it and take it up again for himself."

Then the lesser gods gave up and concluded, "We do not know where to hide it, for it seems there is no place on earth or in the sea that man will not eventually reach." Then Brahma said, "Here is what we will do with man's divinity. We will hide it deep down within man himself, for there he will never look!"

Ever since then, the legend concludes, man has been going up and down the earth, climbing, digging, diving, exploring, searching for something that is already within himself!

ACKNOWLEDGEMENTS

I would like to acknowledge the following people for their contribution to this very personal achievement: the publishing of *Breathe*.

These are the ones who came into my life at just the right time and for the purpose of helping me to get out of my own way so that I may share my story and the lessons that I've learned.

First, for her unwavering dedication, support, strength, love, and patience throughout my journey, I thank my wonderful wife Franca (Piano) Foster.

To my beautiful children, Keeana, Darrell Jr., Giovanni, and Bella, my goddaughters, Camille Leonard and Caila Pinkett, all who have helped me understand the true power and meaning of love and responsibility, thank you.

To Kaci Metzger, my business partner and my right hand, I couldn't have done this without you. Thank you for pushing me to tell my story and for your brilliance in helping me craft my life into the book it's now become.

To my fraternal friends, Sam, Jose, Stan, and Webb, my Omega Psi Phi Brothers that were loyal and persevered to give me unwavering friendship and guidance to see this project through, I would not have made it without you.

To my lifelong friend Sugar Ray Leonard, thank you, Champ, for all the years of Warrior culture and experiences fighting toward the Best in the World. You have greatly enriched my life through friendship and dedication.

To my great friend, Mykelti Williamson, who was key in helping launch my career in Hollywood, thank you for your spiritual counsel, direction, support, and wisdom.

To Will Smith, Jada Pinkett-Smith, and the entire "Team Smith" (Charlie Mack Austin, Pierce Austin, Danielle Demmerella, David Haines, Robert Mata, Judy Murdock, Ralph "Bamm" Saunders, Scot Sardinha, Mike Schaich, Mike Soccio, and Michael "Sparky" Sparks), thank you for accepting me into your family, taking me in as part of the team, and remaining loyal through the years.

To Jana Babatunde-Bey, Clarence Hammond, James Lassiter, Caleeb Pinkett, Omar Rambert, and Harry Smith at Overbrook Entertainment, thank you for all the years of support.

To my agency, CAA—Richard Lovett, Tera Hanks, Simon Green; my literary agent Jason Allen Ashlock; Jared Hoffman at GenerateLA; my editor, Alan Goldsher; EPK Producer Vic Davis and Unit Publicist Cid Swank; my friend Sean Hobart, along with my attorney David Fox at Myman, Greenspan, Fineman, Fox, Rosenburg & Light, LLP: thank you all for your guidance and diligence in seeing this project come to fruition.

Thank you to my clients, students, mentors, other friends, and readers of my story, you have all played a crucial part in my life, helping me to a place of peace and happiness. The things that I've done and written down here, I did it all so that you may know the true power that lies within us all.

"When the Student is Ready, The Teacher Appears."

ABOUT THE AUTHOR

Darrell Foster is the founder and CEO of Omega Bodies, Inc., a Fight and Fitness Corporation that's been serving the entertainment industry for over twenty years. Darrell is the influential and inspirational force behind some of the most successful people in the world. He is a Mentor and Life Coach, as well as a Fight and Fitness Expert, who has worked with notable names in multiple fields of excellence, from World Champion boxer Sugar Ray Leonard to Oscar-nominated actor Will Smith.

Growing up, Darrell spent most of his time reading about and studying boxing and martial arts. This passion led Darrell to work with Sugar Ray Leonard for eighteen years, helping lead him to multiple world boxing titles. Darrell holds black belts in multiple martial arts styles, having traveled to the Far East and trained in the most prestigious dojo in Japan. This vast realm of professional fighting, boxing, mixed martial arts, and self-defense has allowed Darrell to create his own unique training methodology—E2: Enlightenment and Exercise. Darrell uses E2 to help his clients achieve their goals by focusing on the precise conditioning of both the brain and the body.

Aside from working one-on-one with his clients. Darrell's expertise has permeated the film industry in a variety of ways. Working as Stunt Coordinator on major motion pictures, Darrell works to ensure the safety and efficacy of all action sequences/stunts for his films through his precise Action Scene Analysis. Not only responsible for training and transforming Will Smith into Muhammad Ali, Darrell has worked with Hollywood's top talent, including Jada Pinkett-Smith, Antonio Banderas, Nick Cannon, Tyrese Gibson, Virginia Madsen, Alice Braga, Terrence Howard, Mykelti Williamson, Woody Harrelson, Molly Allen, Spencer Breslin, Lolita Davidovich, Duane Martin, Bridget Moynahan, Eddie Murphy, Kevin Phillips, Caleeb Pinkett, Ving Rhames, and Blair Underwood. He has worked also with top film directors and producers, including Gabrielle Muccino and Ron Shelton, and New York Giants owner Steve Tisch.

Equally notable, Darrell is an experienced and trained actor who has studied with acting coaches Tom Todoroff and Aaron Speiser, and has had supporting roles in movies such as Hitch, I Am Legend, and Hancock that have generated billions of dollars in box office profits.

Darrell's influence in filmography includes: Focus, After Earth, Men in Black 3, Seven Pounds, The Human Contract, Hancock, I Am Legend, Pride, The Pursuit of Happyness, Hitch, Hollywood Homicide, I, Robot, The Matrix Revolutions, Bad Boys 2, The Matrix Reloaded, I Spy, Dark Blue, Men in Black 2, Ali, The Kid, and Play It to the Bone, and TV shows Hawthorne and King of Queens.

Visit DarrellFosterOnline.com to learn more.

RECOMMENDED READING

To discover more about Darrell's recommended reading list, visit darrellfosteronline.com/book, where you'll find excerpts from the work featured below, comments from Darrell, and links to download these resources.

The Alchemist by Paulo Coehlo

As A Man Thinketh by James Allen

Aspire: Discovering Your Purpose Through the Power of Words by Kevin Hall

Drive: The Surprising Truth About What Motivates Us by Daniel H. Pink

The Element: How Finding Your Passion Changes Everything by Ken Robinson and Lou Aronica

Excuses Begone!: How to Change Lifelong, Self-Defeating Thinking Habits by Wayne W. Dyer

Man's Search for Meaning by Viktor Frankl

Measure of a Man by Sidney Poitier

Talent is Overrated: What Really Separates World Class Performers From Everybody Else by Geoff Colvin

Think and Grow Rich by Napoleon Hill

PHOTOGRAPHS

The little boy from the beginning of the book.

The family portrait that's so much different than it seems.

Having my family surprise me by borrowing a camper and driving to the Olympic Games in Montreal

With Sugar Ray Leonard and his family during the 1976 Olympic games.

Me with my sports car and a three-piece suit.

My Omega Psi Phi Fraternity Bruhs from the University of Maryland.

Training camp with Sugar Ray. I had to be leaner and
meaner than everyone else.

Training with Sugar Ray on the beaches of Hilton Head, South Carolina, for his bout with Marvin Hagler.

Champ Sugar Ray Leonard with our boxing coach, Mr. Dave Jacobs.

With Woody Harrelson and Antonio Banderas for the film
Play It to the Bone.

During the filming of *Play It to the Bone* with
Antonio Banderas and Woody Harrelson.

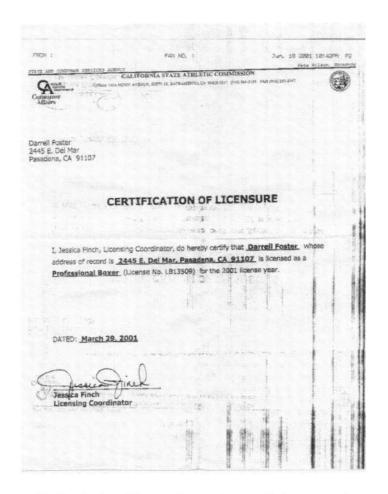

My Professional Boxing license (at age 44) for my work
with training Will Smith for *Ali*.

During the filming of *Ali*.

With Mario Van Peebles and Jeffrey Wright during the filming of *Ali*.

During a grueling training session when Will wrote Ali's name in the snow.

One of the proudest moments of my life: gloving up my hero,
Muhammad Ali.

With the legend, Muhammad Ali when he visited the gym during my
training sessions with Will.

High altitude training in the mountains of Aspen with Will Smith.

Working out with Will Smith on set during the filming of *Men in Black 3*.

Martial arts staff training on the set of *After Earth*.

Working with Will Smith on the set of *After Earth*.

With family and friends before my wedding (L to R: Faye Flora, Leslie Northington, Sam Northington, Me, Piano, Darrell, Jr. and Jose Flora)

Me and Piano on our wedding day, one of the greatest days of my life.

My beautiful bride.

From my wedding—Will Smith, Sugar Ray Leonard, and Darrell Foster, Jr.

The men who stood in my wedding: Darrell Foster, Jr., Will Smith, and
Sugar Ray Leonard.

My son, Darrell Foster, Jr. and **my** daughter, Keeana Foster.

My daughter, Bella and my son, Giovanni.

My wife, Piano, with Bella and Giovanni.

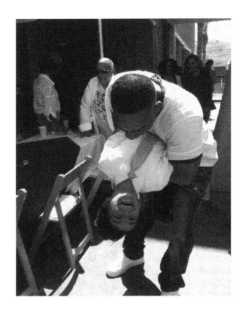

Giovanni having fun with "Uncle Will."

Will supporting my Aikido.

My Aikido family.

The official certification of my black belt in Aikido.

Taking my story and lessons around the world through
E2: Enlightenment and Exercise.

Speaker and Life Coach for those who desire to be the best in the world.

Will Smith wearing the E2: Enlightenment and Exercise wristband.

Printed in Great Britain
by Amazon